# THE HUMANITY OF BUSINESS

# THE HUMANITY OF BUSINESS

Understanding the intriguing parallels between human life cycles and the trajectories of businesses

David Jeb

Copyright © David Jeb 2024

All rights reserved. No part of this publication may be reproduced, distributed, or transmitted in any form or by any means, including photocopying, recording, or other electronic or mechanical methods, without the prior written permission of the publisher, except in the case of brief quotations embodied in critical reviews and certain other noncommercial uses permitted by copyright law.

**Published by:**

Book DNA

books@mediadnagroup.com

# Contents

| | | |
|---|---|---|
| | Acknowledgements | vii |
| | Preface | ix |
| | Introduction | xi |
| 1. | Conception & Birth | 1 |
| 2. | Naming & Identity | 9 |
| 3. | Registration | 15 |
| 4. | Vision & Purpose | 21 |
| 5. | Growth | 27 |
| 6. | Health | 31 |
| 7. | Learning | 39 |
| 8. | Networks & Relationships | 49 |
| 9. | Culture | 63 |
| 10. | Competition & Competitiveness | 67 |
| 11. | Doctors, Experts & Consultants | 71 |
| 12. | Error, Correction & Recourse | 79 |
| 13. | Change | 85 |
| 14. | Code, Image and Brand | 97 |
| 15. | Reproduction | 101 |
| 16. | Posterity and Succession | 105 |
| 17. | Death | 113 |
| 18. | Resurrection | 121 |
| 19. | Soul and Spirit | 125 |

| | | |
|---|---|---|
| 20. | The Hand of God | 129 |
| 21. | The Contrasts | 133 |
| | Conclusion | 137 |

# Acknowledgements

To my university professors at UCU, my former employers and leaders, at UFT, IHK, UNIDO, ITC, CDE, MTAC, mentors in business, partners, investors, employees and team members; Thank you.

To my beloved parents, the late Stephen Johnson Mukwaya and late Grace Kibirige Mukwaya, whose lives in business ignited my passion for entrepreneurship, I am grateful. Their legacy continues to inspire and inform my journey.

To my spiritual instructors, teachers, Bishops, Ministers, Apostle and God's Prophets whose words, covering, guidance and wisdom, enable me to uncover profound spiritual wisdom, I am reverently humbled and accord honour.

To my cherished wife and the cornerstone of my life, Anne Kuteesa, your unwavering love and support have been my strength and solace. You are enough for me; the embodiment of God's blessing in my life. You are crafted for me! It figures.

The concepts woven into this book have been meticulously refined through years of study, dedication, and the refining furnace of personal experiences and credible historical evidence. Each idea reflects a journey marked by observation, deep reflection, and spiritual insight that I have been blessed to experience.

However, it is paramount to recognize that beyond human efforts, it is the gift of God at work within me that has brought forth these revelations. The true author and source of the divine wisdom within these pages is the Lord and God of all life, creation, and creativity. It is His guidance and grace that have channelled these insights through me, shaping the very essence of this work. His divine gift that is at work in me, empowers me to derive knowledge, see wisdom, and to create wealth. I bow in worship and gratitude for His continuous guidance, grace, and the purpose He has bestowed upon me.

Now to all readers and supporters, I present "The Humanity Of Business" with the hope that it inspires a legacy mind-set and fosters enduring, fruitful business relationships and perspectives in your life and endeavours.

With boundless gratitude and reverence,

David Jeb

# Preface

Welcome to "The Humanity of Business," where we embark on a journey that unveils the intriguing parallels between human life cycles and the trajectories of businesses.

Imagine a world where businesses are not just entities but living organisms, evolving through stages akin to our own journey from birth to maturity. In this book, we delve into this concept, exploring how viewing businesses through the lens of human life can unveil profound insights for leaders, guiding them towards sustainable success and resilience.

Just as humans start with a vision and nurture their growth through infancy and childhood, entrepreneurs nurture their businesses, laying foundations of creativity and optimism. As we journey through adolescence, marked by rapid development and risk-taking, businesses too experiment, learn, and build resilience.

The prime of life, for both humans and businesses, symbolizes strength, productivity, and achievement. Here, strategic planning and innovation play crucial roles in maximizing growth and positive impact. Yet, challenges inevitably arise, mirroring life's uncertainties. However, as humans adapt to changes, businesses also reinvent themselves, embracing new strategies or transformations to stay relevant.

The lifecycle of businesses doesn't end at challenges but embraces the concept of resurrection. This phase signifies not just survival but a renaissance, a chance for innovation, purpose, and relevance. Successful leaders understand this analogy, cultivating empathy, resilience, and a holistic view of success beyond financial metrics.

My journey into this exploration began in Uganda, where I witnessed the entrepreneurial spirit but also the short lifespan of businesses.

Through personal experiences and reflections, I unravelled the importance of valuing businesses akin to valuing human life. Join me in uncovering the intricacies of business dynamics intertwined with human experiences, paving the way for enduring success and positive contributions to society.

Let's embark on this transformative journey together.

Warm regards,
David Jeb

# Introduction

The life cycle of humans bears a striking resemblance to the trajectory of businesses, from conception to maturity, facing challenges, and sometimes even experiencing a form of resurrection or renewal. Viewing businesses through the lens of human life offers profound insights for business leaders, guiding them towards sustainable success and resilience in the face of adversity.

At the beginning of their journey, both humans and businesses start with a vision or conception. Just as parents nurture and guide their children through infancy and childhood, entrepreneurs and leaders nurture their businesses, providing the resources, vision, and guidance needed for growth. This early stage is marked by optimism, creativity, and the laying of foundations that will shape future development.

As humans transition through life's stages, encountering challenges and learning from experiences, businesses also navigate a lifecycle marked by growth, setbacks, and opportunities. Adolescence in human life parallels the early growth stages of a business, characterized by rapid development, experimentation, and risk-taking. This phase often involves learning from mistakes, adapting strategies, and building resilience.

The prime of life for both humans and businesses represents a period of strength, productivity, and achievement. Astute business leaders who understand this analogy recognize the importance of strategic planning, innovation, and continuous improvement. They leverage their strengths, talents, and resources to maximize growth, profitability, and positive impact on stakeholders.

However, just as humans face inevitable declines and aging, businesses also encounter challenges such as market saturation, disruptive technologies, economic downturns, or internal inefficiencies. Navigating this stage requires adaptation, reinvention, and, at times, difficult decisions; whether it be restructuring or pivoting strategies to remain competitive and relevant.

The concept of "death" in the lifecycle of businesses can be likened to closures, bankruptcies, or transformations that mark the end of one phase but may lead to new beginnings. While the end of a business as we know it can be painful, it can also pave the way for resurrection or renewal. Successful business leaders embrace change, learn from failures, and leverage experiences to reinvent themselves or start anew, much like a phoenix rising from the ashes.

The analogy of resurrection in business signifies not just survival but a renaissance, a reinvigoration that brings newfound purpose, innovation, and relevance. This phase may involve strategic partnerships, mergers, acquisitions, or transformative initiatives that breathe new life into the organization.

Ultimately, the key takeaway is that businesses, like humans, are dynamic entities with lifecycles that encompass growth, challenges, adaptation, and potential renewal. Business leaders who view their organizations as reflections of humanity cultivate empathy, resilience, and a holistic understanding of success beyond mere financial metrics. They prioritize ethical leadership, stakeholder well-being, and long- term sustainability, positioning their businesses for enduring success and positive contributions to society.

By embracing this perspective, business leaders can navigate the complexities of the business landscape with wisdom, compassion, and a deep understanding of the interconnectedness between human experiences and organizational dynamics.

# 1.

## Conception & Birth

Businesses, like humans, have a unique birth story. Just as humans come into existence through parents, businesses are born from partners who unite to breathe life into their vision. These partners serve as the vital force behind the business, igniting the initial spark that sets the entire journey in motion. Without them, the business would merely remain an idea.

It was the year 2002, and I was a student at Uganda Christian University's Business School. One day, after meticulously crafting my business plans, I caught the attention of my Business instructor, Mr. Isaac Wasswa Katono. He was a paternal figure, gentle yet impactful. Impressed by the distinctiveness of my ideas, he encouraged me with a simple yet profound statement, "Make it a reality, son." It was a moment that stirred something deep within me, as I had never before expressed myself so candidly.

Influenced by a close friend and mentor named David Bukenya, affectionately known as Bunkens, I learned the essence of determination and doing things thoroughly. Bunkens, a former national Rugby hero turned University Librarian, had a knack for inspiring young minds through "The Plus Club." My business plans were shaped with his teachings in mind, and thus, the hypothetical company in my plan was christened Dave & Dave Consultants, a nod to both myself and Bunkens.

After completing my Bachelor's Degree in Business Administration and gaining five years of work experience, I heeded Mr. Katono's charge and founded Dave & Dave Group Ltd. However, Bunkens never officially joined the business, but his influence was profound.

Our conversations over barbecues, pineapples, and country music laid the foundation for the company's ethos and direction. Though he rarely spoke, his words carried weight and wisdom. Operating mostly as a solo venture, Dave & Dave Group thrived in the business landscape, engaging in EU projects, local business diagnostics, and consulting for both local and international entities.

The years from 2007 to 2020 were marked by growth and success until the unforeseen challenges brought by the Covid-19 Pandemic in 2020. Despite relocating our operations to Mauritius due to managerial challenges and other undisclosed factors, the company faced difficulties and was eventually deregistered in 2022.

However, during its active years, Dave & Dave Group contributed significantly to infrastructure projects across Sub-Saharan Africa and played a pivotal role in revitalizing over one hundred and twenty businesses within its network.

Businesses, like humans, start with humble beginnings and uncertainties. They are usually the product of discussions of a few minds and sometimes without definite end in sight, yet, with unwavering dedication and a touch of creativity, they can evolve into something remarkable, leaving a lasting impact on communities and industries alike.

Like many families where the child may end up being raised by only one parent for whatever reason, founding partners in a business may not end up materialising a business together, but then it thrives as would the single parent raised children. The analogy between businesses and humans, especially in the context of conception and birth, is both intriguing and insightful. Just as humans are conceived by parents with unique characteristics and values, businesses are brought to life by visionary partners whose traits and values profoundly influence the business's journey from conception to birth and beyond.

Two visionary partners, akin to expectant parents, come together with a shared dream and a vision for a new business venture. This initial spark of inspiration and collaboration relates to the moment of conception, where possibilities abound, and the foundation for something remarkable is laid. There is a synergy and productivity that can arise from partnership, mirroring the collaborative spirit of business founders.

Just as parents impart values, beliefs, and traits to their children, business founders infuse their venture with their unique qualities, work ethic, and vision. The nature of these "business parents" significantly shapes the culture, goals, and direction of the business as it matures.

When we had just joined the University back in Uganda, we had come to know and be influenced by The Rev. Prof. Dr. Steven Noll, the then University Vice Chancellor fresh out of the United States. He was actually the first Vice Chancellor of the University; a very forward thinking leader and mentor to us then. Having him as V.C. had us feeling, "international", to put it bluntly. He was a man of integrity, values and principle, but kind, attentive and keen on students development. He didn't fail to make a moment for a single student who called on him even for a chat, if he thought you showed potential.

Unbeknownst to us, he had been constantly bombarded

with numerous cases of UCU students menacing local joints and tainting the image of the institution.

I had become very close earlier with two lads in my class, Gordon and Patrick. We were the "Three Musketeers", Ladies were all over us and for good reason.

Gordon was the guy who constantly scored straight A's effortlessly. He was always genuine and courteous. And he would occasionally swing around his Fathers white Toyota Premio. He was the man. Patrick was just, Mr. Cool. Soft spoken, killer smile, wore the latest brands, smelt good, constantly neat haircuts, three showers a day with a change of shoes each time and he wore cool glasses. He couldn't drive though, but it didn't matter in the grand scheme of things. He always got what he wanted.

I was the master strategist. Period! With exotic accents and good looks, strange clothes that captured the eye, a spring in my step, I was hard to ignore. I seemed to know everything; quite the story teller. I said everything so passionately.

So we came up with the "Campus Movie Nights" concept. We brought it to Professor Noll as a possible solution to the mayhem caused by the notorious students. The movie nights would serve as an alternative to student redundancy. We would make some money and put our amateur business skills to the test. He said to us, "You are business students. Make this work. Bring me a business plan in three days."

I laid the strategy, Gordon crunched the numbers and Patrick structured the Promotion. Two days later we came back. I did the presentation of course. Gordon made the ask because somehow he had this responsible trustworthy innocent look. Patrick shook the hand because he was well dressed and looked the part. He always walked around like a supervisor for some reason while Gordon and I did the heavy lifting. But we were a great team.

Professor Noll bankrolled the basics. He gave us the main hall for Fridays and Saturdays, a DVD player, a sound system, screen and even lent us the first movie, "Glory" by Denzel Washington and Morgan freeman amongst other notables. Ours was to promote, publicise, prepare the premises, sell tickets, sell snacks and report. He gave an inaugural speech on opening day and put in a word for us at the general assembly. With help from friends, we hit big the first night and we never stopped, until the university took over. All collections would have to return to Professor who would then direct the splits. He always gave us everything back.

When the university finally took over the project, Professor offered part scholarships for the rest of our education at the university. I very much needed that. Eventually it became free for all students. It changed the university vibe a great deal.

We were distinct individuals who started an enterprise to solve a problem and we were driven by our love for inspirational movies, the image of our university and for me, money and fame. The nuisance reports indeed dwindled down drastically. Each of our values and characters weighed in on the success and shaping of the business.

Founders' values, beliefs, and work ethics shape the culture and direction of their businesses. The values and traits of business founders are relative to the guiding principles that shape their ventures. Founders' resilience and willingness to take risks define the character of their businesses.

Just as a pregnancy involves nurturing and development, the period after business conception is a time of planning, strategizing, and nurturing the idea into a viable business model. Founders invest time, resources, and expertise to nurture their business "baby" and prepare it for the journey ahead.

Like a child's birth marks the culmination of months of preparation, the launch of a business represents the realization of founders' efforts, vision, and aspirations. The business enters the world, ready to make its mark and fulfil its purpose.

There will be risks! There may be failure. It's okay! When a couple conceives, they will experience pain, changed, discomfort, it will cost them, feeding changes, habits, lifestyles etc. Pregnancy is a mysterious process. You don't know if it's a boy or girl, if the baby will be normal and whole, have any health inconsistencies or even come out alive. Baby could be underweight or overweight. Nothing is obvious.

Sometimes the baby comes out but the mother is lost. This goes the same for business. Elon Musk, founder of Tesla and SpaceX, emphasized the importance of taking risks, stating, "Failure is an option here. If things are not failing, you are not innovating enough."

Embracing risk and innovation fuels business growth and evolution.

In essence, the journey of business conception and birth mirrors the human experience in profound ways, highlighting the role of visionary partners as "business parents" who nurture, guide, and shape their ventures with values, wisdom, and faith. As a pregnant mother believes the pregnancy will end in joy, founders must believe and do everything in their power deliberately to ensure they will thrive.

As parents to their children's destinies, founders' values and traits deeply impact the culture, success, and legacy of their businesses, creating a lasting imprint on the entrepreneurial landscape. Partners act as the driving force behind the business, providing the initial spark that sets everything in motion. Without them, the business would never come into existence.

# 2.

## Naming & Identity

Naming a business is like giving a child a name. It's a way to distinguish the business from others and create a brand that people can recognize and remember. A good name can make all the difference in attracting customers and standing out in a crowded marketplace. It's also a depiction of legacy.

The importance of naming in the context of businesses can indeed be likened to the significance of giving a name to a child in human society. Both naming a business and naming a child are profound acts that establish identity, distinguish uniqueness, and contribute significantly to how they are perceived and remembered.

At the core of both endeavours is the concept of identity formation. Just as a person's name becomes an integral part of their identity and how they are recognized by others, a business name serves as its identity in the market. A well-chosen name encapsulates the essence of the business, its values, purpose, and offerings, setting the stage for brand development and customer perception.

The process of naming a business involves careful consideration and strategic thinking, much like how parents deliberate over the name of their child. A business name should ideally be memorable, relevant to its industry or niche, easy to pronounce and spell, and capable of evoking positive associations. These criteria ensure that the name resonates with the target audience and market and contributes to brand recall and recognition.

Moreover, the interdependency between a business's name and its identity is profound. A name is often the first point of contact between a business and its potential customers. It is the gateway through which perceptions, emotions, and expectations are formed.

A strong, cohesive identity that aligns with the business name reinforces brand authenticity, trustworthiness, and differentiation in a competitive landscape. Consider the success stories of iconic brands whose names have become synonymous with their industries or values. Companies like Apple, Google, Nike, and Coca-Cola have not only chosen memorable names but have also built robust brand identities around them. These names evoke emotions, aspirations, and loyalty among consumers, showcasing the power of effective naming in brand building.

Businesses that overlook the importance of naming and identity alignment risk confusion, lack of differentiation, and missed opportunities for brand resonance. A mismatch between a business's name and its identity can lead to disconnects in messaging, brand perception, and customer engagement.

This highlights the critical interplay between a name and identity in shaping brand perception and market positioning. The significance of naming in business extends beyond mere recognition; it influences market competitiveness, customer trust, and long-term success. A well-chosen name becomes a valuable asset that supports marketing efforts, fosters brand loyalty, and contributes to positive brand associations.

It serves as a foundation for brand storytelling, visual identity design, and overall brand experience, reinforcing the business's values and promise to its stakeholders.

### Identity

While a name is important, it is ultimately the essence or identity behind it that truly matters. Similarly, businesses must ensure that their name aligns with their core values and offerings.

Ferrari, for instance, is a brand that resonates with opulence and performance. Owning a Ferrari means acquiring speed, aggression, robustness, and luxury. Conversely, buying a Toyota signifies reliability, affordability, practicality, and value. "The identity of an individual is essentially that which makes him recognizable as an individual." – John Locke. Just as a person's identity is crucial for recognition, a business's identity, encapsulated in its name, is vital for standing out and being remembered in a crowded marketplace.

### Branding and Differentiation

There is a Proverb that says "A good name is more desirable than great riches; to be esteemed is better than silver or gold." The value of a good name cannot be understated. In business terms this translates to a strong brand identity that is esteemed and respected by customers and stakeholders.

Jeff Bezos said, "Your brand is what other people say about you when you're not in the room." A business's name, along with its overall identity, shapes the perceptions and conversations people have about the business.

Until the late 80s, Uganda's automotive market was defined by second-hand imports from Japan and Nairobi, making new cars a luxury for governments and elites. However, Spear Motors Uganda, led by a visionary and charismatic business leader, Sir Gordon Wavamuno, secured brand franchises for Mercedes- Benz, Jeep, and

Mahindra, democratizing access to prestigious global brands.

This move reshaped Uganda's automotive landscape, introducing modern vehicles and raising quality standards. Spear Motors' state-of-the-art showrooms, service centers, and customer support elevated the industry's customer experience, fostering trust and loyalty. Moreover, their focus on technical training enhanced Uganda's automotive expertise, benefiting the industry as a whole.

Beyond business, Spear Motors' social responsibility initiatives in education, healthcare, and environmental sustainability have left a lasting impact on Ugandan society. Their commitment to innovation, integrity, and community welfare solidifies Spear Motors as a transformative force in Uganda's automotive sector, driving progress and inclusivity for all consumers.

### Success and Recognition

"If you don't stand for something, you will fall for anything." – Malcolm X. This quote underscores the importance of having a clear identity and values. A business's name should reflect its core values, helping it differentiate itself and avoid being lost in a sea of competition.

In 1993, after my father's passing, my mother faced a daunting challenge managing his estate amidst legal battles, financial struggles, and demanding distant relatives. Determined to carve her path, she settled all debts, reclaimed titles, and relocated us to a new city. Her goal was clear: to establish her own enterprise. Drawing from her successful retail background at Shell Oils, where she had earned recognition as a top distributor despite being the only woman in that position, she sought to create something entirely her own.

Thus, "Queen's Dairy" was born—a testament to her commitment to quality and excellence. Customers flocked to Queen's Dairy for its unadulterated, farm-fresh cow milk, perfect for all ages.

Despite fierce competition from others who diluted their milk or used questionable practices to cut costs, my mother remained steadfast in delivering pure, unaltered products. Even during power outages, she ingeniously transformed potentially wasted milk into popular yogurt under the brand "Quincy Yoghurt."

While competitors resorted to shortcuts that compromised quality and health, my mother stood firm, declaring, "The Queen's milk stays true." Over time, discerning customers recognized the superiority of Queen's Dairy products, willingly paying higher prices for unmatched quality.

This unwavering commitment not only retained loyal customers but also attracted a niche market willing to pay premium prices. Despite facing periodic losses and intense competition, my mother's dedication to preserving Queen's Dairy's legacy never wavered. Her resilience, ethical standards, and unwavering commitment to quality set Queen's Dairy apart, ensuring its enduring success in the face of challenges. The name was synonymous with true value.

### Legacy and Impact

A well-named business not only establishes its identity but also finds its purpose and impact in the market. Jonah Sachs said once, "Your brand is a story unfolding across all customer touch-points."

A business's name is the beginning of its story, and how that story unfolds across customer interactions shapes its reputation and impact. Just as a person's name carries meaning, history, and personality traits, a business's name encapsulates its essence, values, and aspirations.

The symbiotic relationship between a business's name and its identity emphasizes the importance of thoughtful naming practices in creating impactful brands that resonate with audiences and stand the test of time in dynamic market environments.

This is also true for individuals who live selflessly and leave behind legacies that transcend their time. Siven Selloyee's journey is a testament to the profound impact of identity and humanity. Faced with the choice between spotlighting an international star or a local artist, Siven chose to elevate the latter, sparking a powerful moment of national pride. This decision was more than just a concert—it was a statement of belief in the soul of his people.

When Mauritius erupted in unrest after Kaya's tragic death, Siven's respected voice became the beacon that mediated and restored peace. His actions demonstrated that identity, rooted in empathy and solidarity, can heal divisions and inspire unity. In times of crisis, Siven reminded his nation that true strength comes from within—by embracing who we are and standing together, we can overcome even the deepest conflicts.

Siven Selloyee's choices throughout life reflected his deep love for his country and its people. When faced with a pivotal decision, he ignited a wave of patriotism that resonated across Mauritius. As the nation teetered on the edge of chaos, his calm and thoughtful leadership restored order. His legacy is immortalized in the phrase "Siloy pas Siloy," a lasting symbol in Mauritius that serves to divide right from wrong, reminding all of the enduring power of integrity and moral clarity.

# 3.

# Registration

Once the partners have laid the groundwork, the business is registered through the process of incorporation. This is the official recognition of the business as a legal entity, separate from its owners. It's as if the business is taking its first breath and entering the world with its own identity.

The act of registering a newborn child and incorporating a business indeed serves broader purposes that extend beyond the individual or entity itself. Both processes are integral parts of societal systems designed to ensure accountability, establish legal identities, promote organization, and contribute to the overall functioning and progress of communities and economies.

Examining the parallels between these processes sheds light on their significance in the context of humanity and business.

### Legal Identity and Accountability

Registering a newborn involves creating a legal identity for the individual within a country's system. Similarly, incorporating a business grants it legal recognition as a separate entity from its owners. This legal identity is crucial for accountability, as it establishes responsibilities, rights, and obligations that guide interactions within society and the business environment.

The Enron scandal is a stark reminder of the critical

role that identity and legal frameworks play in ensuring corporate accountability. Their downfall was a result of fraudulent accounting practices, where the company misrepresented its financial status to investors and regulators.

Enron projected an image of success and innovation, but behind the façade, there were unethical practices that went against its stated values. This highlights the importance of aligning a company's identity with its actual practices and values. Loopholes in the legal framework governing corporate governance and financial reporting were exposed. The lack of transparency and accountability allowed unethical behaviour to flourish unchecked. This emphasizes the need for robust legal frameworks that hold companies accountable for their actions and ensure transparency in financial reporting.

The Enron scandal led to calls for greater accountability from corporations, executives, and regulators. It prompted reforms such as the Sarbanes- Oxley Act, which imposed stricter regulations on financial reporting and corporate governance. These measures aimed to enhance transparency, accountability, and integrity within companies.

Individual cases highlight the significance of entity registration, likening it to individuals becoming integral parts of the broader legal framework.

Legal proceedings heavily rely on precedents and historical events, adapting continually to evolving human circumstances. Similarly, corporate activities play a pivotal role in shaping legal frameworks and systems. Therefore, registration, whether for individuals or businesses, establishes them as vital influencers within the dynamic and ever-evolving legal and societal structures.

Legal systems rely heavily on precedents and past

occurrences to make decisions and evolve. When entities are registered, they become part of this historical record and contribute to shaping future legal interpretations and decisions.

Laws and regulations are not static; they evolve to address changing human situations and events. The registration of businesses, for instance, necessitates regulatory frameworks that govern their operations, financial reporting, and interactions with stakeholders. These frameworks adapt in response to corporate occurrences and societal changes.

Registered entities, whether businesses or individuals, become integral parts of economic, social, and legal systems. Their actions and compliance (or lack thereof) influence the effectiveness and fairness of these systems. Corporate scandals, like Enron, often lead to reforms that aim to close regulatory gaps and enhance accountability.
Registration comes with legal responsibilities and obligations. How entities fulfil these responsibilities shapes public perception, regulatory responses, and the overall trust in the system. Ethical and transparent behaviour contributes positively to the legal and societal frameworks.

In essence, registration isn't just a procedural step; it signifies participation in and impact on the larger legal and societal ecosystem. It underscores the dynamic nature of law and its constant evolution in response to human and corporate behaviours and interactions.

Enron Corporation's downfall serves as a stark reminder of the importance of accountability in business. Despite its complex structure and deceptive practices, Enron's legal identity as a corporation held it accountable for financial mismanagement and fraud, leading to legal consequences and regulatory reforms.

### Organizational Structure and Functioning

Registering a new-born within a country's system helps create a structured framework for their upbringing, education, healthcare, and rights protection. Similarly, incorporating a business establishes its organizational structure, governance mechanisms, operational guidelines, and responsibilities towards stakeholders. This structured approach fosters efficiency, transparency, and sustainability in both human and business realms.

The establishment of multinational corporations (MNCs) like Coca-Cola or Toyota showcases how incorporation and structured organizational frameworks enable businesses to operate globally, manage diverse operations, and comply with legal and ethical standards across different jurisdictions.

### Contributions to Societal Progress

Registering newborns ensures that they become part of a society, contributing to its growth, workforce, culture, and progress. Likewise, the incorporation of businesses plays a vital role in economic development, job creation, innovation, and wealth generation within communities and nations.

Successful businesses drive economic activities, support infrastructure development, and enhance living standards through employment opportunities and product/service offerings.

I recently joined a team involved in developing a smart city in Sub-Saharan Africa, driven by the region's abundant gold resources and the promising opportunities within cryptocurrencies and blockchain technology. When we presented our strategy, we encountered a challenge—the government lacked a regulatory framework to oversee such ventures. To proactively address this, they granted us permission to operate within a 'sandbox' environment. This arrangement allows us to launch our business while the government develops the necessary regulatory guidelines based on our operations. It's an innovative approach where both parties learn and collaborate to establish effective governance systems for these cutting-edge initiatives.

The emergence of Silicon Valley as a hub of technological innovation and entrepreneurship underscores the transformative impact of businesses on societal progress. Companies like Apple, Google, and Facebook, born out of innovative ideas and structured incorporation processes, have reshaped industries, created jobs, and propelled economic growth.

### Legal Protections and Rights

Registering a newborn ensures they receive legal protections and access to rights such as healthcare, education, inheritance, and citizenship. Similarly, incorporation grants businesses legal protections, such as limited liability for shareholders, intellectual property rights, contract enforcement, and access to capital markets.

These legal frameworks foster confidence among stakeholders and support long-term investment and growth. The global pharmaceutical industry's reliance on patent protections highlights how legal frameworks, including incorporation and intellectual property rights, incentivize innovation and investment in research and development. Companies like Pfizer or Moderna secure patents for life-saving drugs, encouraging continuous advancements in healthcare.

The registration of newborns within societies and the incorporation of businesses serve as fundamental processes with far-reaching implications for humanity and economic ecosystems.

By providing legal identities, fostering accountability, enabling structured functioning, contributing to societal progress, and ensuring legal protections, these processes play pivotal roles in shaping individual lives and driving business innovation, resilience, and impact on a larger scale. Registration and incorporation shape successful enterprises and contribute to societal well-being and progress.

# 4.

## Vision & Purpose

A famous proverb says, "where there is no vision, the people cast off restraint". It carries profound wisdom applicable not only to nations but also to humans and businesses alike. This proverb emphasizes the importance of having a clear purpose, direction, and long-term goals in order to maintain order, discipline, and progress.

At a fundamental level, humans share a deep connection with this proverb. Individuals without a vision or clear goals in life often struggle with motivation, focus, and self-discipline. Without a sense of purpose or direction, people may feel lost, aimless, or prone to making impulsive decisions.

This lack of vision can lead to a life of stagnation, where potential remains untapped, and personal growth is hindered. Similarly, businesses embody this proverb in their pursuit of success and sustainability. A company without a clear vision or mission statement risks losing its competitive edge, organizational coherence, and employee engagement.

A well-defined vision serves as a guiding light, aligning the efforts of employees toward common objectives, fostering innovation, and enhancing customer satisfaction. Without this vision, businesses may struggle to adapt to changing market dynamics, lose sight of their core values, or fail to capitalize on emerging opportunities. To sidetrack a little, we can observe that the relevance of this proverb extends to the broader context of societal development and governance. Nations that lack a collective vision or a shared sense of purpose often experience social discord, political instability, and economic setbacks.

A nation's vision encompasses its aspirations, values, and goals, shaping policies, institutions, and societal norms. When a nation fails to articulate and pursue a unifying vision, it risks fragmentation, polarization, and a breakdown of social cohesion.

In essence, the biblical proverb underscores the universal need for vision, purpose, and direction in various domains of human endeavour. It highlights the power of foresight, planning, and proactive leadership in fostering individual fulfilment, organizational excellence, and societal progress. Whether at the personal, organizational, or national level, embracing a clear vision not only prevents chaos and disorder but also unlocks potential, fuels innovation, and paves the way for a brighter future.

### Escobar & Hitler: A Case for Aimless Power, Deadly Vision

The Medellín Cartel led by Pablo Escobar rose to prominence in the 1970s and 1980s, gaining immense wealth and power through drug trafficking. He built a robust business or organisation. However, despite their initial success, the Medellín Cartel ultimately crumbled due to a lack of a sustainable vision beyond immediate profits and a centralized leadership figure.

Pablo Escobar's leadership style was characterized by ruthlessness, violence, and a focus on short-term gains. The cartel's operations were driven by greed and the pursuit of power without a clear long-term strategy or vision for sustainable growth. This lack of foresight and coherent vision led to internal conflicts, external pressure from law enforcement agencies, and ultimately the downfall of the cartel after Escobar died in 1993.

Contrastingly, the Nazi movement under the leadership of Adolf Hitler, though not a business, provides a stark example of a destructive vision that almost conquered the world. Hitler's leadership was characterized by a strong vision of racial superiority, territorial expansion (Lebensraum), and ideological domination. The Nazi regime mobilized a nation and orchestrated one of history's most devastating wars based on Hitler's grand vision of a racially pure German empire. The Nazi movement's success in mobilizing resources, technology, and manpower was fueled by Hitler's charismatic leadership and ability to articulate a compelling vision that resonated with many Germans at that time.

However, the catastrophic consequences of this vision, including genocide, war crimes, and widespread destruction, highlight the danger of unchecked power and an extremist vision devoid of moral and ethical constraints. We see the crucial role of vision, leadership, and the ethical dimension in shaping the outcomes of human endeavours.

While a visionary leader can inspire greatness and achieve remarkable feats, the absence of a responsible, ethical vision can lead to chaos, destruction, and eventual downfall. These historical examples underscore the importance of leadership that balances ambition with ethical considerations and a sustainable, long-term vision for the betterment of society whether in business or human perspectives.

### Tata Tuition: A Case for Vision, Power and Purpose

One of the most prominent examples of a massively successful business in India that was built by a visionary leader and continues to have a significant impact is the Tata Group, founded by Jamsetji Tata.

He was a visionary industrialist and philanthropist who laid the foundation for what would become one of India's largest and most diversified business conglomerates. He had a clear vision of industrializing India and contributing to its economic and social development.

Tata's vision was rooted in industrialization and self-reliance. He believed in building indigenous industries that could compete globally. His vision led to the establishment of several pioneering ventures, including Tata Steel, India's first integrated steel plant, which played a crucial role in India's industrial growth.

Beyond business success, Tata was committed to improving the lives of communities. He founded educational institutions like the Indian Institute of Science and Tata Institute of Fundamental Research, laying the groundwork for scientific and technological advancements in India. The Tata Group also initiated social welfare programs, healthcare initiatives, and rural development projects.

The Tata Group's success and longevity can be attributed to its adherence to ethical business practices, long-term strategic planning, and a commitment to corporate social responsibility. Under subsequent leaders like J.R.D. Tata and Ratan Tata, the group expanded globally while maintaining its core values and vision.

Today, the Tata Group is a diversified conglomerate with businesses spanning sectors such as steel, automobiles, IT services, hospitality, and more. It continues to be a major contributor to India's economy, providing employment, driving innovation, and investing in sustainable development projects.

The Tata Group's journey exemplifies how a visionary

leader with a clear vision, ethical values, and a focus on societal impact can build a business empire that withstands the test of time and positively influences multiple communities and industries.

# 5.

## Growth

Just like humans need to be fed to grow and thrive, businesses need resources and support to succeed. This can come in the form of funding, mentorship, and a strong network of partners and suppliers. Without these essential nutrients, a business will struggle to survive and reach its full potential.

Moreover, for businesses, the parallel to food for humans would be resources like capital, human talent, technology, and market access. These are essential elements that businesses need to thrive and grow. Just as food provides energy and nutrients for human growth and sustenance, these resources provide the necessary fuel and support for businesses to develop, innovate, and expand.

Sure, here are live examples for each aspect from different continents:

Silicon Valley is a prime example of how capital investment fuels business growth. Venture capital firms like Sequoia Capital and Andreessen Horowitz have funded numerous tech startups such as Airbnb, Uber, and Zoom, contributing to their rapid growth and global expansion.

German engineering companies like Siemens and Volkswagen are known for their skilled workforce. Germany's emphasis on technical education and apprenticeship programs has helped these companies maintain a competitive edge in manufacturing and innovation.

Samsung Electronics is a leading example of how technological innovation can drive business growth. Through continuous R&D investments, Samsung has become a global leader in smartphones, semiconductors, and consumer electronics, contributing significantly to South Korea's tech industry.

Dangote Group, founded by Aliko Dangote, illustrates how market access and leveraging can fuel business expansion. Dangote Group operates in various sectors like cement, sugar, and oil refining, leveraging Nigeria's large domestic market and expanding its presence across Africa and beyond.

In most cases, capital, personnel, technology, and market access are the food that play crucial roles in driving business growth across continents. Businesses, like humans, have the capacity to grow and evolve over time. Just as individuals learn from their experiences and adapt to new challenges, businesses can also expand their operations, increase their market share, and improve their overall performance.

**Apple Inc**

Apple's transformation from a niche computer company to a global tech giant is a testament to strategic growth. Under the visionary leadership of Steve Jobs, Apple revolutionized industries with iconic products like the iPod, iPhone, and iPad. Its focus on innovation, user experience, and ecosystem integration propelled its growth, making it one of the most valuable companies globally. As with human potential, businesses can achieve remarkable growth through visionary leadership, innovation, and strategic adaptation to market trends.

## Kodak

Kodak's decline from a photography powerhouse to bankruptcy serves as a cautionary tale. Despite pioneering digital photography technology, Kodak failed to capitalize on its invention due to internal resistance and a reluctance to disrupt its lucrative film business. This short-sightedness led to missed opportunities, loss of market share, and eventual decline. Stagnation as can be found amongst individuals is not strange to businesses. Without embracing change, businesses that resist innovation and fail to adapt risk retardation and irrelevance.

## Amazon

Amazon's evolution from an online bookstore to a global e-commerce, cloud computing, and digital streaming behemoth showcases sustained growth. Jeff Bezos' customer-centric approach, strategic acquisitions, and investments in logistics and technology propelled Amazon's expansion into diverse markets, solidifying its position as a tech giant.

What started as an online bookstore in 1994 has now grown into one of the largest e-commerce companies in the world, offering a wide range of products and services to customers globally.

Through strategic acquisitions, innovative technology, and a customer-centric approach, Amazon has continuously evolved and expanded its business to meet the changing needs of consumers Businesses can achieve continuous growth by prioritizing customer satisfaction, strategic diversification, and leveraging technology for competitive advantage. The journey of human development often mirrors the trajectory of businesses, with both experiencing periods of growth and stagnation.

## Nokia

Nokia's dominance in the mobile phone industry eroded due to complacency and missed opportunities. Despite early success with mobile phones, Nokia failed to innovate rapidly in the smartphone era, allowing competitors like Apple and Samsung to surpass it. This led to a significant decline in market share and Nokia's eventual exit from the phone business. Failing to adapt to changing technological landscapes can lead to business retardation, highlighting the importance of agility and foresight in staying competitive.

## Tesla Inc

Tesla's journey from a niche electric car start-up to a leader in sustainable energy and transportation exemplifies exponential growth. Elon Musk's bold vision, relentless innovation, and focus on sustainability propelled Tesla's rise.

The company's disruptive approach to electric vehicles, renewable energy solutions, and autonomous technology has reshaped industries. Businesses can achieve rapid growth by challenging norms, pursuing disruptive innovation, and aligning with emerging trends and societal needs.

Much like humans, businesses can experience phases of growth or retardation depending on their strategies, leadership, adaptability, and response to market dynamics. Learning from both successes and failures is essential for businesses to navigate challenges, seize opportunities, and strive for sustained growth, contributing to economic vitality and innovation in society.

# 6.

## Health

Businesses, like humans, are complex organisms that can experience periods of robust health and times of vulnerability. The analogy between the health of businesses and the health of humans provides valuable insights into the challenges, strategies for resilience, and the importance of proactive management in both realms.

Firstly, just as humans require a holistic approach to maintain good health, businesses also need a comprehensive strategy that addresses various aspects such as financial stability, market adaptation, leadership, and internal dynamics. Neglecting any of these areas can create vulnerabilities, much like how neglecting physical, mental, or emotional well-being leads to health issues in humans.

Consider the concept of resilience. Healthy individuals can better withstand stressors and recover from setbacks. Similarly, resilient businesses have mechanisms in place to weather economic downturns, changes in consumer preferences, or technological disruptions. This resilience often comes from diverse revenue streams, strong financial management, and a culture of innovation and adaptability.

Preventative measures are also crucial in both contexts. Just as individuals undergo regular health check-ups and adopt healthy habits to prevent illnesses, businesses must conduct regular assessments of their operations, monitor industry trends, and invest in continuous learning and development.

In 2010, the Dave & Dave Group Ltd spearheaded a transformative initiative, deploying 19 newly trained consultants commissioned by the ITC's Enterprise Competitiveness Section. Supported by funding from CDE, the project aimed to conduct 100 comprehensive business diagnostics within a specified timeframe.

Each consultant undertook the responsibility of analyzing four to five companies, delving deep into their operational dynamics. The outcomes were profound and far-reaching. Through meticulous assessments, it became evident that several SMEs were operating far removed from their core business offerings, resulting in a misalignment with their target markets. Furthermore, some businesses lacked a clear Unique Selling Proposition (USP), reflecting a crucial need for market differentiation strategies.

One of the project's significant achievements was the overhaul of marketing systems across multiple SMEs. This strategic revamping not only enhanced market reach but also realigned businesses with their intended customer segments, fostering stronger positioning and competitive advantage.

Moreover, the diagnostics uncovered operational inefficiencies stemming from misaligned employee roles and responsibilities. Addressing these internal challenges led to a broader restructuring of business strategies for many participating entities. It catalyzed a profound introspection, prompting a strategic realignment to rectify weaknesses and capitalize on untapped opportunities.

The project's impact extended beyond mere diagnostics; it catalyzed a paradigm shift in how these SMEs approached their business operations. It underscored the importance of strategic positioning, market alignment, and operational excellence in sustaining long-term competitiveness.

Overall, the collaboration between Dave & Dave Group Ltd, ITC's Enterprise Competitiveness Section, and CDE yielded tangible results, empowering SMEs to navigate complexities, optimize resources, and chart a course towards sustainable growth and success.

Proactive measures can help identify potential weaknesses early on and mitigate risks before they escalate.

The role of leadership in maintaining the health of businesses mirrors the importance of personal responsibility in maintaining individual health. Effective leaders set the tone for organizational culture, foster collaboration, and make strategic decisions that steer the company toward sustainable growth. The project was championed in partnership with Uganda Women Entrepreneurial Association Ltd (UWEAL), which was headed at the time by Jennifer

Mwijukye, a vibrant and forward-thinking entrepreneur herself. The 100 SUE'S were part of their membership. Conversely, poor leadership can lead to internal conflicts, lack of direction, and ultimately, organizational decline.

Furthermore, the interconnectedness of businesses within an economic ecosystem reflects the interdependence of organs and systems within the human body. A disruption in one part can have cascading effects on others.

For instance, supply chain disruptions can impact production, sales, and customer satisfaction, highlighting the need for resilience and contingency planning at every level.

The 2020 COVID-19 pandemic and global lockdown caused a worldwide shortage in the supply of microchips for automotive manufacturing. As a leading global automaker, Ford relies heavily on microchips for various vehicle components, including engine management systems, infotainment systems, and advanced driver-assistance features. The shortage disrupted Ford's production lines, leading to widespread production slowdowns and, in some cases, temporary factory shutdowns.

During the height of the microchip shortage, Ford was forced to reduce production volumes across multiple vehicle models. This not only impacted their ability to meet consumer demand but also resulted in increased lead times for vehicle deliveries.

As a result, Ford experienced revenue losses and supply chain strains, highlighting the interconnectedness of global industries and the vulnerability of supply chains to external disruptions.

Additionally, Ford had to navigate pricing pressures as reduced supply coincided with increased consumer demand for vehicles, leading to a competitive market landscape with limited inventory availability. These challenges underscored the complex interdependencies within the automotive ecosystem and emphasized the need for agile supply chain strategies and resilience in the face of unforeseen disruptions.

Another aspect of the analogy lies in the concept of seeking help and professional guidance when needed. Just as individuals consult doctors, therapists, or specialists for health concerns, businesses benefit from engaging with consultants, financial advisors, legal experts, and industry mentors to address specific challenges, gain new perspectives, and implement effective strategies.

Ethical considerations also play a significant role in both spheres. Ethical business practices are akin to ethical principles guiding healthcare, emphasizing transparency,

## THE HUMANITY OF BUSINESS

fairness, and responsibility toward stakeholders. Violations of ethical norms can erode trust, tarnish reputation, and lead to long-term damage, highlighting the importance of integrity in sustaining business health.

The analogy between the health of businesses and humans underscores the complexity, interdependence, and dynamic nature of both domains. By adopting a proactive, holistic approach, prioritizing resilience, fostering strong leadership, and upholding ethical standards, businesses can navigate challenges, thrive in competitive environments, and contribute positively to economic and societal well-being, much like individuals striving for optimal health contribute to a vibrant and resilient society.

As businesses grow, they may encounter challenges and setbacks that can make them "fall sick." This could be due to changes in the market, internal conflicts, or other external factors. Like humans, businesses need to adapt and seek help when they are struggling to stay afloat.

Businesses facing challenges and setbacks can indeed be likened to humans falling sick and needing doctors. History is replete with such scenarios which have helped demonstrate the relationship.

### Market Changes and Adaptation

Blockbuster, once a giant in the video rental industry, failed to adapt to the digital streaming era. This failure to recognize and respond to market changes led to its downfall, while Netflix, by embracing online streaming, became a dominant force. Just as humans need to adapt to changing environments, businesses must continually assess market trends and adapt their strategies to stay competitive.

### Internal Conflicts and Management Issues

Uber faced internal turmoil due to allegations of a toxic

workplace culture, leading to the resignation of its CEO Travis Kalanick. This situation significantly impacted Uber's brand image and operations. Internal conflicts can weaken a business just as health issues can affect an individual. Seeking professional guidance and implementing necessary changes are crucial for recovery.

### Financial Struggles and Restructuring
General Electric's Decline. Once a symbol of American corporate might, General Electric faced financial troubles due to a combination of factors including mismanagement, high debt, and declining market share in key sectors. It underwent significant restructuring efforts to regain stability. In the face of financial difficulties, businesses need strategic planning and financial expertise to navigate through tough times and regain financial health.

### Technological Disruptions and Innovation
Nokia, a leading mobile phone manufacturer, missed the smartphone revolution, clinging too long to its traditional phone designs. This allowed competitors like Apple and Samsung to dominate the market.
Innovation and embracing of emerging technologies keeps businesses relevant. Just as humans seek medical advice to improve health and stay healthy, businesses must seek expertise in technology and innovation as well as stay abreast of potential threats in the business arena or playfields.

### Legal and Compliance Challenges
Volkswagen faced severe consequences after it was discovered that they had installed software in their diesel cars to cheat emissions tests. This scandal led to massive fines, loss of consumer trust, and legal battles. Compliance

issues can severely impact a business's health. Legal counsel and implementing ethical practices are essential for long-term sustainability Businesses face critical challenges akin to human health issues. Seeking help, whether through consulting, restructuring, or strategic partnerships, is vital for businesses to recover and thrive, just as individuals seek medical professionals for diagnosis and treatment when facing health challenges.

# 7.

# Learning

Learning is a fundamental concept and trait shared between humans and businesses, showcasing the interconnectedness and parallel journeys of growth, adaptation, and improvement. Let's delve into the relationship between learning in human beings and learning within business organizations, highlighting key similarities, processes, and outcomes that underscore the importance of continuous learning for personal and organizational success.

### Learning as a Core Human Trait
Human beings are inherently curious and adaptable creatures, wired to learn from experiences, observations, and interactions with the environment. From infancy to adulthood, humans engage in a lifelong journey of learning, acquiring knowledge, skills, and perspectives that shape their understanding of the world and their ability to navigate it effectively.

Learning encompasses formal education, practical experiences, social interactions, introspection, and exposure to diverse ideas and cultures. It involves cognitive processes such as perception, memory, reasoning, and problem-solving, reflecting the complex nature of human intelligence and learning capabilities.

## Learning in Business Organizations

Just as individuals learn and grow, businesses and organizations also engage in continuous learning processes to stay competitive, innovative, and responsive to evolving market dynamics. Learning within businesses involves acquiring new knowledge, adapting to changes in technology and industry trends, improving operational efficiencies, and fostering a culture of innovation and creativity.

Business learning extends across various levels, from individual skill development to organizational learning that involves knowledge sharing, collaboration, and strategic decision-making based on data-driven insights.

## Human and Business Learning: The Relativity

Adaptation to Change: Both humans and businesses must adapt to changing environments, whether it's technological advancements, market disruptions, or societal shifts. Learning enables individuals to acquire new skills, update knowledge, and embrace change, while businesses leverage learning to innovate, pivot strategies, and seize emerging opportunities.

Problem-Solving and Decision-Making: Learning enhances problem-solving abilities in humans, enabling them to analyse situations, generate solutions, and make informed decisions. Similarly, businesses rely on learning processes to address challenges, optimize processes, and make strategic decisions that drive growth and competitiveness.

Feedback and Improvement: Feedback mechanisms play a crucial role in human learning and business learning alike. Individuals benefit from feedback to assess performance, identify areas for improvement, and refine skills. In businesses, feedback loops from customers, stakeholders, and performance metrics inform continuous improvement efforts, product/service enhancements, and customer satisfaction initiatives.

Innovation and Creativity: Learning fuels innovation and creativity in both humans and businesses. Individuals explore new ideas, experiment with solutions, and think critically, fostering innovation in various fields. Businesses cultivate a culture of learning and innovation through research and development, cross-functional collaboration, and investment in employee training and development programs.

### Learning Culture and Organizational Success

Organizations that prioritize learning and development foster a learning culture that empowers employees, encourages knowledge sharing, and drives collective growth. A learning culture promotes employee engagement, retention, and productivity, leading to improved performance and competitive advantage. Businesses that invest in learning initiatives, research, mentorship programs, and continuous skill development not only adapt to market changes but also create a resilient and agile workforce capable of driving innovation and achieving strategic goals.

### Learning as a Continuous Journey

Both human learning and business learning are ongoing processes that require commitment, curiosity, and adaptability. Embracing a growth mind-set, seeking opportunities for learning and development, and valuing continuous improvement are essential principles that drive personal and organizational success. Learning enables individuals to reach their full potential, businesses to stay relevant and innovative, and societies to progress and thrive in a dynamic global landscape.

### Strife Masiyiwa

As a personal favourite of mine, the story of a businessman who turned around a struggling business through learning and transformation in Africa; Strive Masiyiwa, the founder and executive chairman of Econet Wireless Group teaches us much. In the late 1990s and early 2000s, Econet Wireless faced significant challenges in Zimbabwe's telecommunications sector due to regulatory hurdles, economic instability, and intense competition.

Masiyiwa navigated through these challenges by initially launching Econet Wireless Zimbabwe in the face of opposition and legal battles. Despite setbacks and adversity, he persevered and gained valuable insights into the complexities of operating in a volatile business environment. His experiences running Econet Wireless Zimbabwe provided him with a deep understanding of market dynamics, regulatory frameworks, customer preferences, and technological advancements in the telecommunications industry.

Using the lessons learned from running Econet Wireless Zimbabwe, Masiyiwa strategically expanded the Econet Wireless Group across several African countries, including Zambia, Botswana, Lesotho, and Nigeria. He leveraged his knowledge of regulatory challenges, financial management, and customer-centric strategies to transform Econet Wireless into a leading telecommunications and technology group in Africa.

Masiyiwa's emphasis on innovation, investment in infrastructure, and commitment to social impact initiatives such as mobile banking and rural connectivity played pivotal roles in Econet Wireless Group's turnaround and subsequent success. By continuously learning from both successes and setbacks, Masiyiwa demonstrated how adaptive leadership, resilience, and strategic vision can revitalize a struggling business and position it for sustainable growth in challenging business environments.

Ultimately, the relationship between learning in humans and learning in business organizations reflects the shared principles of adaptation, problem-solving, feedback-driven improvement, innovation, and continuous growth. Organizations can harness the power of knowledge, creativity, and resilience to navigate challenges, seize opportunities, and achieve sustainable success in an ever-changing world.

### Idi Amin Dada and the Asians

Idi Amin Dada's expulsion of Indians and Asians from Uganda in the 1970s was a significant event that had lasting effects on both the country's economy and its social fabric. Idi Amin's decision to expel these communities stemmed from a combination of political, economic, and ideological factors.

His ascent to power in Uganda was fuelled by a complex interplay of factors. Political instability and internal tensions created fertile ground for his rise, as he strategically maneuvered to consolidate power amidst a volatile environment. Amin's vision was to wield significant control, particularly in vital economic sectors such as trade and commerce, shaping policies to assert authority and maintain influence.

Central to Amin's narrative were economic grievances among certain segments of the Ugandan populace. There existed a widely held perception that Indians and Asians held disproportionate economic sway, sparking resentment and demands for economic restructuring. Amin capitalized on these sentiments, weaving them into a nationalist and pan-African ideology that resonated with many Ugandans. His rhetoric centred on empowering Ugandan citizens and reducing perceived foreign economic dominance, aligning with broader movements for independence and self-determination across Africa during that era.

The repercussions were economic and social in nature. The expulsion of Indian and Asian business owners, professionals, and skilled workers led to a significant disruption in various sectors such as manufacturing, trade, finance, and services.

Many businesses were left abandoned or taken over by the government, causing economic decline and loss of expertise. Socially and culturally, communities that had long been part of Uganda's diverse fabric were uprooted blatantly. It led to displacement, loss of homes and livelihoods, and fractured social ties.

Among the notable businesspeople affected by the expulsion was Manubhai Madhvani, a prominent Ugandan industrialist of Indian descent. The Madhvani Group, founded by Manubhai's father, was a leading player in Uganda's sugar industry and diversified into various sectors including textiles, agriculture, and hospitality. The expulsion forced Manubhai Madhvani and his family to leave Uganda, resulting in significant disruptions to their businesses and the broader economy.

General Idi Amin wanted to assert control, redistribute economic resources, and promote a nationalist agenda. However, the consequences of this decision were far-reaching, leading to economic setbacks, social upheaval, and the loss of valuable expertise and investments. In the aftermath of Idi Amin's regime and subsequent leadership changes, Uganda under President Yoweri Kaguta Museveni recognized the need to reverse these policies and attract back the expelled communities for the benefit of the country's economic recovery and development. The return of business leaders like Manubhai Madhvani and others fostered a shift towards inclusivity, reconciliation, and the recognition of the contributions of diverse communities to Uganda's progress and prosperity.

Today, much of Uganda's business community has been revamped. Moreover, there is a discussion ongoing in Uganda to adopt Indians as a special tribe in Uganda and to be regarded as Citizens.

The leadership traits and policies of President Yoweri Museveni exemplify a leader who, despite an extended tenure, has shown a capacity to learn from past mistakes and craft a future-oriented approach. Museveni's governance reflects an understanding of the crucial roles of security, economic stability, social inclusivity, and technological advancement.

Regardless of one's political stance, it is evident that Museveni has implemented significant reforms that underscore the importance of continuous learning and improvement across various sectors. One of Museveni's key focuses has been on national security. Having experienced the turmoil of past conflicts, Museveni prioritized stabilizing the country through a robust security apparatus. This focus has not only helped to maintain peace within Uganda but also contributed to regional stability in East Africa. The establishment of disciplined armed forces and effective intelligence systems has been crucial in preventing insurgencies and maintaining order.

Museveni has also spearheaded economic reforms aimed at fostering stability and growth. In the late 1980s and 1990s, Uganda's economy was in dire straits, plagued by hyperinflation and a crumbling infrastructure. Learning from these challenges, Museveni implemented liberalization policies, promoted foreign direct investment, and embraced economic diversification. The introduction of structural adjustment programs with the support of international financial institutions helped to stabilize the economy, reduce inflation, and spur growth. Despite criticisms of uneven growth patterns, these policies laid the groundwork for sustained economic development.

Understanding the importance of social inclusivity without compromising national identity, Museveni's administration has made strides in improving access to education and healthcare. The Universal Primary Education (UPE) program, introduced in 1997, was a landmark reform aimed at providing free primary education to all Ugandan children. This policy significantly increased school enrollment rates and improved literacy levels, contributing to the overall social development of the country.

Recognizing the transformative potential of technology, Museveni has also pushed for advancements in ICT. Uganda was one of the first countries in Africa to liberalize its telecommunications sector, leading to widespread mobile phone adoption and internet accessibility.

The government's commitment to ICT development is evident in initiatives like the National Backbone Infrastructure (NBI) project, which aims to extend internet connectivity across the country. These efforts have enhanced communication, business operations, and access to information for many Ugandans.

President Museveni's approach to governance demonstrates the importance of learning from past mistakes and continuously improving. His policies reflect an understanding that building a resilient and prosperous nation requires adapting to new challenges and leveraging lessons learned. For instance, the shift from a state-controlled economy to a liberalized market was a direct response to the failures of previous economic models. Similarly, the focus on education and technology stems from recognizing the need for a skilled and connected populace to drive future growth.

Museveni's tenure offers valuable insights into the importance of leadership that prioritizes learning and adaptability. His focus on security, economic stability, social inclusivity, and technological advancement showcases a commitment to building a strong foundation for national development. Businesses and other entities can indeed draw lessons from Museveni's approach, understanding that continuous improvement and learning from past experiences are essential for long-term success and resilience.

# 8.

## Networks & Relationships

Making friends in the business world is crucial for success. Building strong relationships with suppliers, customers, and other businesses can open up new opportunities and help a business thrive. These connections, also known as backward and forward linkages, can provide valuable support and resources that can help a business grow and succeed.

During the global financial crisis of 2008, many businesses faced immense challenges, including General Electric (GE), one of the world's largest conglomerates. GE was heavily involved in financial services through its GE Capital division, which faced significant losses due to the economic downturn.

In this difficult situation, GE leveraged its strong relationships with other businesses to navigate through the crisis. One notable example is when Warren Buffett's Berkshire Hathaway invested $3 billion in GE preferred shares in 2008. This investment not only provided GE with much-needed capital during a turbulent time but also signaled to the market that a renowned investor like Buffett had confidence in GE's long-term prospects.

Furthermore, GE also strengthened its relationships with various government agencies and financial institutions to access additional funding and support. Through strategic partnerships and collaborations, GE managed to stabilize its financial position and gradually recover from the effects of the financial crisis.

A well-connected and resourceful business like GE used its relationships with investors, government entities, and financial institutions to weather a severe economic downturn and emerge stronger in the long run.

On the flip side, Lehman Brothers was a global financial services firm with extensive connections and relationships in the financial industry. Despite its strong network and relationships, the company ultimately couldn't harness them to save itself from a tough situation during the same 2008 crisis.

Lehman Brothers had long-standing relationships with other financial institutions, including banks, investment firms, and regulatory bodies. However, when Lehman faced a liquidity crisis and mounting losses due to its exposure to risky mortgage-backed securities, its network wasn't able to provide sufficient support to prevent its downfall.

Lehman Brothers attempted to seek a buyer or a bailout from other financial institutions and government entities. Potential buyers like Barclays and Bank of America were initially interested in acquiring Lehman, but the deals fell through due to concerns about Lehman's financial health and the broader economic situation.

The financial crisis eroded trust and confidence in Lehman Brothers, making it challenging for the company to leverage its relationships effectively. Counterparties became wary of dealing with Lehman, leading to liquidity problems and a rapid decline in market confidence.

Regulatory constraints, market conditions, and the interconnectedness of the financial system played significant roles in Lehman Brothers' inability to turn its relationships into salvation. The lack of a coordinated rescue effort and the prevailing panic in the financial markets exacerbated Lehman's situation.

Despite having a strong network and relationships within the financial industry, Lehman Brothers couldn't overcome the systemic challenges and market dynamics that contributed to its collapse. A company might have good relations and networks but once these are not activated to benefit, businesses will take a hit where they would have hit big.

### Marriage, Partnerships & Mergers

The comparison between marriage and business partnerships as collaborative endeavours is a compelling one, highlighting the intricate dynamics involved in both institutions. Partnerships and collaborations are another avenue through which businesses achieve growth and create new opportunities.

The partnership between Apple and Nike to create the Apple Watch Nike+ is a testament to leveraging complementary strengths to innovate and capture new market segments. Tim Cook, CEO of Apple, emphasized the value of collaboration by stating, "Great things in business are never done by one person. They're done by a team of people."

This sentiment underscores the importance of strategic alliances and synergies in achieving mutual goals. By combining Apple's expertise in technology with Nike's understanding of athletic performance and branding, the partnership produced a product that resonated with fitness enthusiasts and tech-savvy consumers alike, showcasing the power of collaborative innovation.

At its core, marriage embodies a union between individuals based on shared values, goals, and mutual support. Similarly, business partnerships are forged with the aim of achieving common objectives, pooling resources, and leveraging complementary strengths. One historical example that exemplifies this synergy is the partnership between Nelson Mandela and Oliver Tambo, who co-founded South Africa's first black legal firm in the 1950s.

This partnership was not only a professional collaboration but also a deep friendship rooted in a shared vision of justice and equality. Their enduring bond and collective efforts were instrumental in the struggle against apartheid and the advancement of human rights in South Africa.

Effective communication is a cornerstone of successful marriages and business partnerships alike. Just as spouses must communicate openly and honestly to navigate challenges and strengthen their bond, business partners must maintain transparent and constructive dialogue to address issues, make informed decisions, and foster trust.

European business history presents the partnership between the brothers Theo and Vincent van Gogh to offer valuable insights. While Vincent's artistic genius is widely celebrated today, it was Theo's unwavering support, financial backing, and promotional efforts as an art dealer that sustained Vincent during his tumultuous artistic journey.

Their correspondence, filled with candid discussions about art, life struggles, and ambitions, reflects the depth of their partnership and the crucial role of effective communication in their shared endeavours. Mutual respect is another critical aspect shared between successful marriages and business partnerships. Respecting each other's perspectives, contributions, and boundaries nurtures a positive and harmonious environment conducive to growth and collaboration.

The partnership between Elon Musk and his early collaborators in ventures like PayPal and Tesla illustrates the power of mutual respect and trust. Despite facing numerous challenges and setbacks, Musk's ability to inspire, empower, and collaborate with his teams has been instrumental in realizing ambitious technological innovations and business successes.

Shared values form the foundation upon which enduring marriages and business partnerships thrive. Aligning on core principles, ethics, and long-term objectives fosters a sense of unity, purpose, and resilience. The partnership between Adidas founders Adolf Dassler and Rudolf Dassler exemplifies this notion. Adidas was founded by Adolf Dassler and his brother Rudolf Dassler in 1949.

Before that, the Dassler brothers had started a shoe company together in the 1920s, but they split ways due to personal and business conflicts. Adolf Dassler continued with his part of the business, which eventually became Adidas, while Rudolf Dassler went on to found Puma. Despite their eventual business rivalry and split, their shared passion for sports, innovation, and quality craftsmanship laid the groundwork for what would become one of the world's leading athletic footwear and apparel brands.

The relationship between Adolf and Rudolf Dassler does bear some similarities to human relationships like marriage and divorce, especially in the context of business partnerships. Just like in personal relationships, business partnerships can experience conflicts, disagreements, and ultimately separations. These events can be driven by various factors such as differing visions, goals, or management styles.

In the case of the Dassler brothers, their split led to the creation of two successful sports footwear companies,

Adidas and Puma, which have since become global brands. It's interesting how personal dynamics and conflicts can shape the trajectory of businesses and industries. Adaptability is a hallmark of both successful marriages and businesses, especially in navigating evolving challenges and seizing opportunities.

Flexibility, openness to change, and the ability to learn and grow together are vital for sustainability and resilience. Consider the partnership between South African Breweries (SAB) and global beverage giant Anheuser-Busch InBev (ABI). Through strategic mergers, acquisitions, and market adaptations, SAB evolved from a local brewery to a key player in the global beer industry, showcasing the importance of adaptability and strategic partnerships in a dynamic business landscape.

Investment, whether in the form of time, effort, resources, or innovation, is essential for the growth and sustainability of both marriages and businesses. Just as couples invest in their relationship through quality time, emotional support, and shared experiences, businesses invest in research, development, talent, and market expansion to remain competitive and relevant.

Unilever, a multinational consumer goods company with roots in both Europe and Africa, underscores the significance of long-term investment and strategic planning in building a diversified and resilient business portfolio. The company emphasizes long-term investment and strategic planning for business success. They operate in various sectors such as food and beverages, home and personal care, and refreshments, giving them a diversified portfolio that can withstand market fluctuations.

This approach helps them adapt to changing consumer preferences, economic conditions, and regulatory environments in different regions globally. By focusing on sustainability, innovation, and responsible business practices, Unilever continues to strengthen its position as a leader in the consumer goods industry while contributing positively to society and the environment. This attempts to drive us into key aspects of successful marriages, cognizant of course, the uniqueness of each relationship and the dynamics thereof.

No single size fits all. The values examined here could cut across acceptably if one chose to see it that way without claiming absolutes:

### Commitment
Just as marriages require commitment from both partners, businesses need commitment from their stakeholders, including employees, investors, and customers. Long-term success often stems from a strong commitment to shared goals and values.

### Communication
Effective communication is crucial in both marriages and businesses. Clear communication fosters understanding, resolves conflicts, and ensures everyone is aligned towards common objectives.

### Adaptability
Both marriages and businesses must be adaptable to changing circumstances. Flexibility and the ability to evolve with the times are key to overcoming challenges and staying relevant.

### Trust
Trust is the foundation of any successful relationship, whether personal or professional. Businesses build trust

through transparency, reliability, and ethical practices, just as couples do through honesty and dependability.

### Investment
Just as couples invest time, effort, and resources in their relationship, businesses invest in research, development, and innovation to stay competitive and grow.

### Resilience
Both marriages and business partnerships encounter ups and downs. Resilience, perseverance and the ability to learn from setbacks are vital for long-term sustainability.

To sum it up, the analogy between marriage and business partnerships offers profound insights into the interconnectedness of human relationships and collaborative endeavours. As seen from real historical examples from companies in South Africa and Europe, we can appreciate the universal principles of effective communication, mutual respect, shared values, adaptability, and investment that underpin success and sustainability in both realms.

Just as marriages and partnerships evolve and face challenges, so too do businesses, highlighting the enduring relevance and complexity of these human interactions across different contexts and eras.

### Mergers and Acquisitions: Lessons from Marriage and Human Relations

Mergers and acquisitions (M&A) are complex processes in the business world, involving the consolidation of companies or the purchase of one company by another. These strategic maneuvers are akin to the dynamics found in human relationships, particularly in marriage and interpersonal connections. Exploring the parallels between

M&A activities and human relations offers valuable insights into the challenges, strategies, and outcomes involved in both realms.

Firstly, the decision to engage in a merger or acquisition mirrors the choice to enter into a committed relationship or marriage. In both cases, careful consideration of compatibility, shared values, and long-term goals is essential. Just as individuals assess their compatibility before committing to a relationship, businesses evaluate factors such as cultural fit, strategic alignment, and potential synergies before pursuing M&A deals.

DDG Holdings' acquisition of AGC, a gold refinery in Mauritius, proved to be a strategic move. AGC, with its expertise in refining gold to high-grade products, had faced stagnation due to unrealized output goals and overheads. DDG Holdings, an investment company with strong financial collaterals, saw an opportunity to revitalize AGC's operations.

The merger brought together AGC's refining capabilities and DDG's forward linkages with Dubai-based bullion banks, ensuring a steady offtake for AGC's products. With DDG's management having roots in Africa, they were well-positioned to meet supply quotas and expand market reach. Today, the merged entity is poised to establish the largest Bullion

Bank in Africa and collaborate with Singaporean trade platforms to develop the largest gold repository on the continent. Communication plays a pivotal role in both M&A transactions and human relationships. Effective communication fosters understanding, alignment of expectations, and the resolution of conflicts. Clear and transparent communication channels are crucial during the pre-merger phase to address concerns, mitigate uncertainties, and build trust among stakeholders.

Similarly, open and honest communication is foundational in nurturing healthy human relationships, promoting trust, intimacy, and mutual respect. The integration phase following an M&A deal parallels the early stages of a relationship or marriage. Both require adjustments, compromises, and a shared vision for the future. Integrating different corporate cultures, systems, and processes in M&A transactions mirrors the merging of individual lifestyles, preferences, and habits in personal relationships.

Successful integration efforts prioritize collaboration, empathy, and a focus on common goals, ensuring a smooth transition and maximizing the value of the union. Challenges often arise in both M&A activities and human relations, requiring resilience, adaptability, and problem-solving skills.

Unexpected obstacles, cultural clashes, and divergent priorities can test the strength of a newly merged entity or a committed relationship. Flexibility and the ability to navigate uncertainties with a growth mindset are crucial for long-term success and sustainability.

Trust is another fundamental element shared between M&A transactions and human relationships.

Building and maintaining trust is a continuous process that hinges on reliability, transparency, and integrity. Trustworthy leadership and consistent actions are paramount in M&A deals to reassure stakeholders and foster post-merger cohesion. Similarly, trust forms the cornerstone of healthy human relationships, fostering emotional intimacy, loyalty, and a sense of security. Lastly, the outcomes of M&A activities and long-term relationships are influenced by strategic planning, investment in growth, and a shared vision.

Just as businesses invest in synergies, innovation, and

market expansion post-merger, individuals in relationships invest in personal growth, mutual support, and shared experiences to nurture a fulfilling partnership over time.

### GlaxoSmithKline (GSK)

The merger between Glaxo Wellcome and SmithKline Beecham to form GlaxoSmithKline (GSK) in 2000 offers a compelling narrative on the significance of compatibility and shared goals in corporate mergers. This case illustrates that, akin to individuals assessing compatibility before committing to a relationship, businesses must evaluate strategic alignment meticulously before merging. The process underscores the necessity of clear communication and a shared vision, particularly during the critical integration phase, mirroring the foundational stages of a strong personal relationship.

Glaxo Wellcome and SmithKline Beecham, two major players in the pharmaceutical industry, recognized the potential benefits of merging their operations. Both companies shared a commitment to innovation, research, and development, which provided a strong basis for strategic alignment. This compatibility was crucial in fostering a smooth transition and integration, as it allowed both entities to build on their mutual strengths and shared objectives. The evaluation of strategic alignment is a vital step in the merger process. For Glaxo Wellcome and SmithKline Beecham, this meant carefully considering how their combined resources, expertise, and market presence could be leveraged to create a more competitive and innovative entity. This strategic foresight is akin to individuals in a relationship assessing long-term compatibility and shared life goals before making a commitment.

Once the decision to merge was made, the importance

of clear communication and a shared vision became paramount. Effective communication ensured that all stakeholders, including employees, investors, and customers, were aligned with the merger's objectives and understood the benefits. This clarity helped in managing expectations and reducing uncertainty, which is essential for maintaining trust and morale during the integration process.

The integration phase of the GSK merger was marked by a concerted effort to create a unified corporate culture. This involved harmonizing business practices, systems, and values from both companies to ensure a cohesive and collaborative working environment. Much like the early stages of building a strong relationship, this required patience, mutual respect, and a commitment to working through differences.

The shared vision of GSK centred on becoming a global leader in pharmaceuticals and healthcare. This common goal provided a clear direction and purpose, motivating employees and guiding strategic decisions. The ability to articulate and pursue a shared vision is critical in any merger, as it helps to align efforts and resources towards achieving common objectives.

The merger between Glaxo Wellcome and SmithKline Beecham to form GSK underscores the importance of compatibility and shared goals in corporate mergers. By thoroughly evaluating strategic alignment, ensuring clear communication, and fostering a shared vision, businesses can navigate the complexities of integration more effectively. This approach, analogous to building a strong personal relationship, is essential for realizing the full potential of a merger and achieving long-term success.

**DaimlerChrysler**

The merger of Daimler-Benz and Chrysler in 1998 to form DaimlerChrysler stands as a prominent example of the complexities that can arise when merging companies with distinct corporate cultures. This case illustrates the vital importance of adaptability, empathy, and effective communication in ensuring a harmonious union, akin to the dynamics of a marriage.

Daimler-Benz, a German automotive giant, was characterized by its conservative, hierarchical, and meticulous approach to business. In contrast, Chrysler, an American car manufacturer, was known for its dynamic, risk-taking, and informal culture.

These stark cultural differences created significant challenges in management styles and business practices once the two companies attempted to integrate.

The process of integration, which involves aligning processes, systems, and cultures, proved to be particularly arduous for DaimlerChrysler. The differing operational methods led to misunderstandings and conflicts, hampering the realization of synergies that are often the primary motivation behind mergers. Employees from both sides frequently found it difficult to collaborate effectively, as the expected harmony between German precision and American innovation was elusive.

Adaptability and empathy are crucial in any merger, as they facilitate the adjustment to new ways of working and foster an understanding of the other company's perspective. Unfortunately, these elements were markedly lacking in the DaimlerChrysler merger. A prevailing 'us vs. them' mentality took root, and insufficient efforts were made to build a unified corporate culture that embraced and integrated the strengths of both companies. This absence of mutual understanding and flexibility further deepened the divide between the two corporate cultures.

Effective communication is another critical factor in the success of a merger. It helps manage expectations and build trust among employees. However, DaimlerChrysler suffered from poor communication strategies, leading to widespread confusion and uncertainty. The lack of clear, consistent communication exacerbated the cultural clashes and impeded the integration process, ultimately contributing to the failure of the merger.

The marriage analogy is particularly fitting, as merging companies, like spouses, must navigate their differences with patience and understanding. They need to create a shared vision and work collaboratively towards common goals, fostering a sense of unity and cooperation. Without these elements, a merger is likely to face significant challenges, as evidenced by the DaimlerChrysler experience. The merger failed to achieve its intended outcomes and ultimately led to the separation of the companies in 2007.

The DaimlerChrysler merger underscores the critical importance of cultural compatibility, adaptability, empathy, and effective communication in corporate mergers. It serves as a cautionary tale that highlights the potential pitfalls of merging distinct corporate cultures without adequately addressing the human and cultural aspects of such a union.

# 9.

## Culture

The culture within a business organization plays a crucial role in shaping its identity, direction, and leadership style. Just as individuals are influenced by their cultural backgrounds and values, businesses also operate within a cultural context that guides their strategies, decisions, and relationships.

In India, the concept of joint families and strong family bonds often leads to a scenario where individuals, even from the working class, continue to live with their parents even into their 30s. This setup provides a support system that extends beyond financial assistance to include emotional and social support. This familial support can also extend to business ventures, where skills, knowledge, and even businesses themselves are passed down from one generation to another. For example, traditional family businesses like textiles, jewellery, or small-scale manufacturing often thrive due to this intergenerational continuity and support.

On the other hand, in many African cultures, there's an expectation for young adults to become independent early in life. This can be seen in the emphasis on leaving the parental home and starting one's own life, including finding work and renting accommodation.

Entrepreneurship in Africa often emerges from this sense of independence and necessity, where individuals have to create opportunities for themselves due to limited formal employment options. Examples include tech start-ups in Nairobi's Silicon Savannah or innovative agricultural ventures in rural areas, driven by individuals' ingenuity and resourcefulness.

These cultural differences not only shape individual lifestyles but also influence the dynamics and origins of businesses within these regions. Japan is known for its strong emphasis on harmony, consensus-building, and long-term relationships. Japanese businesses often prioritize group cohesion and collective goals over individual achievements. This is reflected in their management practices, such as participatory decision-making processes (known as "ringi-seido") and lifetime employment commitments.

Companies like Toyota exemplify this cultural influence, where teamwork, continuous improvement (Kaizen), and respect for hierarchy are deeply ingrained. Toyota's leadership style emphasizes a collaborative approach, where managers act as mentors and facilitators rather than authoritative figures. This cultural framework has contributed to Japan's reputation for quality, innovation, and resilience in the global market.

In Germany, the business culture is characterized by efficiency, precision, and a strong work ethic. German companies often value technical expertise, thorough planning, and adherence to rules and regulations. The concept of "Mittelstand," referring to small and medium-sized enterprises (SMEs) with a focus on specialization and innovation, is a notable aspect of the German business landscape. Companies like BMW and Siemens exemplify German business culture through their emphasis on engineering excellence, high-quality products, and long-term strategic planning. German leadership tends to be structured, with clear hierarchies and decision-making processes, yet also values employee welfare through initiatives like vocational training and work-life balance.

In contrast, New Zealand presents a unique blend of cultural influences, combining elements of indigenous Maori values with Western business practices. The Maori concept of "whanaungatanga" (meaning relationships and interconnectedness) is increasingly integrated into New Zealand's business culture, emphasizing collaboration, inclusivity, and sustainability. Companies like Fonterra, a global dairy cooperative, embody these values by engaging with local communities, promoting environmental stewardship, and fostering a sense of belonging among employees. New Zealand's business leadership often embraces a more flexible and adaptive approach, encouraging innovation, diversity, and social responsibility.

Overall, one can notice how culture shapes the identity, direction, and leadership styles of businesses. Whether it's the collective orientation of Japanese firms, the efficiency-driven ethos of German companies, or the inclusive and sustainable practices in New Zealand, cultural values deeply influence organizational strategies, decision-making processes, and relationships within businesses. Understanding and leveraging cultural dynamics can be a key driver of success for businesses operating in diverse global contexts.

# 10.

## Competition & Competitiveness

In the competitive world of business, it's important to recognize that not everyone will be a friend. Competitors can be fierce rivals, constantly vying for the same customers and market share. Businesses need to be strategic and innovative to stay ahead of the competition and carve out their own niche in the market.

The humanity perspective in this aspect will allow one to navigate the Competitive Business World and this will facilitate ones capacity to develop effective strategies for Success. In the fast-paced and cutthroat world of business, competition is inevitable. As businesses strive to attract customers and increase market share, they must be prepared to face fierce rivals who are constantly vying for the same opportunities. In order to thrive in this competitive landscape, it is essential for businesses to be strategic, innovative, and adaptable.

### Understanding the Competitive Landscape

The concept of competition in the business world will position business owners at a point of competition. There are different types of competitors that businesses may encounter, from direct competitors who offer similar products or services, to indirect competitors who cater to the same customer needs in a different way. By understanding the competitive landscape, businesses can better position themselves to stand out and succeed.

Just as businesses face competition in the marketplace, humans encounter competition and competitiveness in various aspects of their lives. The concept of competition is ingrained in human society, shaping interactions and outcomes across different domains.

Take education for instance. Students compete for grades, scholarships, and opportunities. Just as businesses vie for market share and customer loyalty, students strive to excel academically and distinguish themselves from their peers. This competition can foster innovation, motivation, and continuous improvement, much like how businesses innovate to stay ahead in the market. In the professional world, individuals compete for jobs, promotions, and recognition.

This competition drives people to enhance their skills, develop new talents, and showcase their unique value propositions. Much like businesses positioning themselves in the market, individuals position themselves within their respective industries, leveraging their strengths and differentiators to advance their careers.

In sports and athletics, competition is at the forefront. Athletes compete not only against opponents but also against their own limits and previous performances. This competitive spirit pushes athletes to train harder, set higher goals, and strive for excellence. Just as businesses aim to outperform competitors, athletes aim to outperform themselves and achieve new milestones.

Moreover, social dynamics often involve competition for social status, recognition, and acceptance. People compete for attention, approval, and influence within social circles. This competition can lead to the development of social skills, networking abilities, and emotional intelligence, akin to how businesses build relationships and networks to expand their reach and influence.

In essence, competition and competitiveness are fundamental aspects of human life, mirroring the dynamics observed in the business world. By understanding and navigating these competitive landscapes, individuals can learn valuable lessons in resilience, adaptability, and strategic thinking.

Businesses strive to stand out and succeed amidst competition, humans too must harness their strengths, differentiate themselves, and continuously evolve to thrive in competitive environments. In today's interconnected and socially conscious world, the imperative for businesses to compete ethically and responsibly mirrors the ethical standards expected of individuals.

Just as people are expected to uphold moral values and integrity in their actions, businesses must prioritize ethical conduct in their competitive endeavours. Ethical competition entails fair practices, transparency, respect for stakeholders, and a commitment to social and environmental responsibility. In recent years, Facebook has faced significant scrutiny and criticism for its handling of user data and privacy concerns. The case also brought about revamps in the data management with tech companies. Policies were reflected in behavioural changes across most companies. Whenever you browse anywhere, you are required consent.

The Cambridge Analytica scandal, which came to light in 2018, revealed that Facebook had allowed the personal data of millions of users to be harvested without their consent by a third-party political consulting firm. This data was then used for targeted political advertising during elections, raising serious ethical questions about user privacy and the responsibility of tech companies to safeguard sensitive information.

This case underscores the need for businesses, especially those in the tech industry, to prioritize ethical conduct in their operations. Customers and stakeholders expect companies to handle their data responsibly and transparently, and failure to do so can lead to legal consequences, loss of trust, and damage to reputation. Businesses that prioritize ethical conduct not only comply with regulations and industry standards but also build stronger relationships with customers based on trust and integrity. In the long run, ethical behaviour is not just a moral imperative but also a strategic advantage for businesses in today's competitive landscape.

By embracing ethical competition, businesses not only build trust and credibility with their customers but also contribute positively to society, fostering a sustainable and equitable business ecosystem for the benefit of all stakeholders. This is the humanity of Business and The Business of Humanity.

# 11.

## Doctors, Experts & Consultants

As a young professional at Uganda Finance Trust, a local bank that originated as a cooperative of women in business, I witnessed a significant transformation within the organization. They transitioned from being solely a credit entity to becoming a deposit-taking institution and eventually evolved into the bank they are today. During this transformative period, we engaged the expertise of a consultant named Peter Okaulo. Peter not only played a crucial role in guiding us through this journey but also took on the mantle of CEO for a time.

I vividly remember attending a training event where Peter shared a memorable definition of a consultant: "A consultant is one who tells you the time according to your watch." This simple yet profound statement encapsulates the essence of consulting. It highlights the consultant's role in leveraging existing knowledge, understanding the client's perspective, and providing tailored guidance and solutions. Peter's insight resonated deeply with us as we navigated through strategic decisions and organizational changes. His ability to work collaboratively, build on our strengths, and align strategies with our vision was instrumental in our successful transition and growth.

Today, as I reflect on those times, I appreciate the wisdom in Peter's words and the impact of effective consulting on our journey of evolution and success at

Uganda Finance Trust. Much like individuals seek medical expertise when faced with illness, businesses often seek the counsel of consultants to navigate challenges and achieve optimal performance. These seasoned professionals offer invaluable insights and strategic frameworks that can guide businesses through complex landscapes, enabling them to thrive amidst dynamic market shifts.

With the adept support of consultants, businesses can transcend obstacles and harness opportunities, evolving into agile and competitive entities within their industries. This symbiotic relationship mirrors the fundamental human need for guidance and support during critical junctures, underscoring the parallel between businesses and personal endeavours.

Just as individuals rely on the expertise of doctors for wellness and recovery, businesses leverage the specialized knowledge of consultants to fortify their strategies, adapt to change, and realize their full potential. This synergy exemplifies the profound impact that strategic collaboration and professional counsel can have on organizational growth and resilience in today's ever-evolving business landscape.

Choosing the right consultants for businesses is relative to humans selecting the right doctors for their health concerns. Three things are key while making these choices: expertise, trustworthiness, and compatibility in both scenarios, and there are always consequences of choosing the wrong consultants or doctors.

Imagine a business as a person seeking professional advice and guidance, just like an individual would seek medical expertise from a doctor. Just as humans have different healthcare needs, businesses have unique challenges and goals that require specialized knowledge and support.

## The Specialist vs. the General Practitioner

When it comes to healthcare, individuals often seek specialists for specific health issues. Similarly, businesses may require consultants with specialized expertise in areas such as finance, marketing, technology, or human resources. Choosing a consultant who is a "specialist" in the relevant field ensures tailored solutions and in-depth insights that address specific business needs effectively. On the other hand, opting for a "general practitioner" consultant for complex or niche areas may result in generic advice that falls short of solving critical business challenges.

## Trust and Reputation

Just as humans trust their health to reputable doctors with proven track records, businesses prioritize consultants with established credibility and reputation. Positive reviews, client testimonials, and industry recognition play a significant role in building trust between businesses and consultants. A trustworthy consultant instils confidence, provides reliable advice, and collaborates effectively with the business's internal teams, fostering a productive and successful partnership.

## Compatibility and Communication

Compatibility between a patient and their doctor is crucial for effective healthcare management. Similarly, businesses thrive when there is good rapport and communication between consultants and internal stakeholders. A consultant who understands the business's culture, values, goals, and communication style can integrate seamlessly into the organization, facilitate change management, and drive meaningful outcomes. Misalignment in communication or working styles can lead to misunderstandings, delays, and suboptimal results.

## Diagnosing Problems and Prescribing Solutions

Just as doctors diagnose health issues and prescribe treatments, consultants diagnose business challenges and recommend solutions. A skilled consultant conducts thorough assessments, analyses data, identifies root causes, and proposes actionable strategies that align with the business's objectives. However, choosing the wrong consultant can be likened to receiving a misdiagnosis or inappropriate treatment in healthcare, leading to wasted resources, missed opportunities, and potential setbacks for the business.

## Continuity of Care and Long-Term Relationships

In healthcare, continuity of care ensures ongoing monitoring, follow-ups, and adjustments to treatment plans. Similarly, businesses benefit from consultants who offer ongoing support, monitoring of implemented strategies, performance evaluations, and adjustments based on evolving needs and market dynamics. Building long-term relationships with trusted consultants fosters collaboration, knowledge transfer, and sustained business success over time.

## Learning from Mistakes

Just as humans may learn from experiences with healthcare providers, businesses can learn from past experiences with consultants. If a business chooses the wrong consultant initially, it can analyse what went wrong, reassess its needs, and make informed decisions to choose the right consultant in the future. Learning from mistakes ensures that businesses become more discerning and strategic in selecting consultants who genuinely add value to their operations and growth strategies.

The analogy between businesses choosing consultants and humans selecting doctors sheds light on the critical factors of expertise, trust, compatibility, communication, and learning from experiences. By approaching the consultant selection process with care, diligence, and a sense of partnership, businesses can benefit from valuable insights, innovative solutions, and collaborative relationships that contribute to their long-term success and well-being in the dynamic business landscape.

### The Importance of Consultants

Consultants play a crucial role in helping businesses create their future by providing expert advice and guidance. They bring a fresh perspective and specialized knowledge that can help businesses navigate challenges and seize opportunities. Starbucks faced challenges with declining market share in the early 2000s, leading them to seek external expertise to revitalize their business.

One of the key consultants Starbucks engaged during this period was Jim Donald. Jim Donald, an experienced retail executive, was brought in as a consultant in 2002 and later became the CEO of Starbucks in 2005. Jim Donald played a pivotal role in implementing operational changes and strategic initiatives that contributed to Starbucks' turnaround during his tenure. His focus on operational efficiency, customer experience improvements, and expansion strategies helped reinvigorate the brand and regain market momentum.

Starbucks also opened arms to Howard Schultz, the former CEO and founder of Starbucks. Schultz returned to the company in 2008 as CEO, leading initiatives to refocus on core values, product innovation, and customer engagement, further contributing to Starbucks' resurgence and sustained growth. These consultants, along with internal leadership and strategic adjustments, played significant roles in Starbucks' transformation and resurgence as a leading global coffee retailer.

### The Ottoman Empire: Lessons

In history, the Ottoman Empire provides an intriguing example of the impact of consultants and advisors on governance and administration. During the Ottoman era, the empire reached its peak in the 16th and 17th centuries, spanning vast territories across Southeast Europe, Western Asia, and North Africa. The Ottomans employed various advisors and consultants known as "Viziers" to assist in matters of governance, law, finance, and military strategy.

One notable example is Ibrahim Pasha, who served as the Grand Vizier (chief minister) under Sultan Suleiman the Magnificent. Ibrahim Pasha played a crucial role in implementing administrative reforms, modernizing the Ottoman bureaucracy, and strengthening the empire's military capabilities. His strategic counsel and leadership contributed to the Ottoman Empire's stability, expansion, and cultural flourishing during the period known as the "Golden Age" of the Ottoman Empire.

### The United Arab Emirates

In a modern perspective, the transformation of the United Arab Emirates (UAE) from a desert country to a global economic powerhouse is a remarkable success story facilitated by strategic consulting and expertise from around the world. The UAE, particularly Dubai and Abu Dhabi, has experienced unprecedented growth and development in various sectors such as finance, tourism, real estate, and technology.

Consultants and advisors from diverse backgrounds have played instrumental roles in shaping the UAE's vision, policies, and strategic initiatives. For instance, Dubai's transformation into a world-class business and tourism hub was spearheaded by visionary leadership under the guidance of consultants specializing in urban planning, economic development, and infrastructure.

One prominent consultancy firm that contributed significantly to Dubai's development is McKinsey & Company. McKinsey advised Dubai's leadership on economic diversification strategies, investment promotion, and governance reforms. Their recommendations supported initiatives like the establishment of free zones, development of infrastructure projects such as Dubai International Airport and Jebel Ali Port, and the launch of innovative initiatives like Dubai Internet City and Dubai Media City.

Additionally, consultants from sectors like finance, architecture, hospitality, and technology have collaborated with UAE entities to drive innovation, attract foreign investment, enhance tourism experiences, and promote sustainable development practices.

The success of the UAE as a global city and economic hub underscores the value of strategic partnerships with consultants and experts who bring diverse perspectives, best practices, and global insights to facilitate growth, resilience, and competitiveness in an ever-evolving world. Through visionary leadership, strategic planning, and leveraging external expertise, the UAE has transformed its landscape and economy, becoming a model for rapid development and modernization on the global stage.

Consultants, if carefully selected will play a vital role in helping businesses evolve and thrive in a constantly changing marketplace. By leveraging their expertise and guidance, businesses can overcome challenges, seize opportunities, and reach their full potential. Just like humans seek out doctors when they are sick, businesses can turn to consultants for advice and support to ensure their long-term success. As legendary business people have shown us, the right support can make all the difference in transforming a business into a powerhouse in its industry.

# 12.

## Error, Correction & Recourse

"To err is human..." Alexander Pope. Businesses, like humans, are complex entities operating within dynamic environments, and they are prone to making mistakes and corrections as they navigate challenges, adapt to changes, and pursue growth and sustainability.

Examining the relations between business mistakes and human errors provides valuable insights into organizational learning, resilience, and the pursuit of continuous improvement.

Errors in judgment, lapses in communication, or misinterpretation of information are common human mistakes. These can lead to misunderstandings, conflicts, or suboptimal outcomes in personal or professional contexts. Similarly, businesses make mistakes in strategic decisions, operational processes, product development, or customer interactions. These mistakes may result in financial losses, reputational damage, or missed opportunities in the market.

Cognitive biases, lack of information, emotional factors, or external pressures can contribute to human errors. For example, confirmation bias may lead individuals to overlook contradictory data, resulting in flawed decision-making. In the business realm, factors such as market volatility, competitive pressures, organizational culture, or inadequate risk assessment can lead to mistakes. For instance, a company may underestimate market demand for a new product, leading to inventory issues and revenue loss.

Mistakes in personal or professional life can have emotional, financial, or social consequences. Learning from mistakes often involves reflection, accountability, and taking corrective actions to mitigate negative outcomes and prevent recurrence. Business mistakes can impact stakeholders such as investors, employees, customers, and communities. They can erode trust, affect market share, and influence long-term sustainability. Effective management of mistakes includes transparent communication, proactive problem-solving, and strategic adjustments to regain confidence and competitiveness.

Learning from mistakes is a fundamental aspect of personal growth and development. It involves acknowledging errors, seeking feedback, acquiring new skills or knowledge, and implementing changes to improve future outcomes.

Similarly, businesses engage in corrective actions and organizational learning processes. This may include conducting root cause analyses, revising strategies or policies, investing in employee training, or leveraging feedback from customers and stakeholders to enhance products or services. Resilience is the ability to bounce back from setbacks, learn from challenges, and adapt to changing circumstances. Individuals cultivate resilience through self-awareness, problem-solving skills, and a positive mind-set. Business resilience involves agile decision-making, risk management practices, diversification strategies, and innovation capabilities. Resilient businesses are adept at learning from failures, seizing opportunities, and evolving their strategies to stay competitive and relevant in evolving markets.

## Continuous Improvement

The concept of continuous improvement, often associated with methodologies like Kaizen, emphasizes incremental progress, feedback loops, and a culture of learning and innovation. In the business context, continuous improvement frameworks such as Six Sigma, Lean Management, or Total Quality Management promote systematic approaches to identifying and correcting errors, optimizing processes, and enhancing overall performance.

DBS Bank, headquartered in Singapore, provides a compelling illustration of learning from mistakes and continuous improvement. In 2016, DBS faced a major technology outage that disrupted online banking services for customers. This incident highlighted vulnerabilities in their IT infrastructure and customer service protocols.

However, DBS responded by conducting a thorough review, investing heavily in upgrading their systems, enhancing cybersecurity measures, and implementing robust contingency plans. The bank's proactive approach not only restored customer trust but also positioned DBS as a leader in digital banking innovation, winning accolades for its customer-centric approach and technological advancements. BlackBerry, once a dominant player in the smartphone market, experienced significant setbacks due to market shifts and competitive pressures. The company's initial focus on physical keyboard devices limited its adaptability to touch-screen smartphones, leading to declining market share and financial struggles.

However, BlackBerry undertook a strategic transformation, diversifying into software and security solutions. Learning from past mistakes, refocusing its strengths, and embracing innovation, had BlackBerry evolve into a leading provider of cybersecurity and enterprise software solutions, showcasing resilience and strategic adaptation in the face of industry challenges.

Thai Union Group, a global seafood company based in Thailand, encountered issues related to labour practices and sustainability in its supply chain. Reports of unethical labour practices and environmental concerns raised scrutiny and criticism from stakeholders. Thai Union responded with a comprehensive sustainability strategy, investing in responsible sourcing practices, improving working conditions, and promoting marine conservation initiatives.

Acknowledging past mistakes, collaborating with stakeholders, and implementing sustainable business practices, influenced the Thai Union to transform its reputation and became a leader in ethical seafood sourcing, demonstrating the power of corrective actions and responsible business practices.

Ecobank Transnational Incorporated, with a presence across West and Eastern Africa, faced challenges related to governance and operational efficiency in the past. The bank experienced issues such as regulatory compliance, risk management, and customer service gaps.

However, Ecobank took decisive measures to strengthen its governance frameworks, enhance risk management practices, and invest in technology to improve service delivery. Through a concerted effort to address weaknesses, embrace digital transformation, and foster a culture of accountability, Ecobank regained investor confidence, expanded its market reach, and contributed to financial inclusion and economic growth in the region.

History is replete with such cases globally that illustrate the universal nature of challenges faced by businesses and the importance of learning from mistakes to drive positive change and sustainable growth. Whether in the finance sector, technology industry, or seafood supply chain, businesses across diverse regions share common principles of resilience, adaptation, and continuous improvement in navigating complexities and achieving long-term success.

The relationships between business mistakes and human errors highlight the shared principles of learning, resilience, and continuous improvement. Just as individuals learn from their mistakes to grow and adapt, businesses leverage experiences, data, and feedback to refine their strategies, operations, and offerings. Embracing a culture of accountability, learning, and proactive problem-solving enables both humans and businesses to thrive amidst challenges and uncertainties, fostering innovation, resilience, and long-term success. This is the humanity of Business.

# 13.

## Change

Change is an intrinsic and vital principle that resonates deeply within both human lives and business environments, serving as a catalyst for growth, adaptation, innovation, and success. Change is multifaceted and is an essential element that brings positive transformations to individuals and businesses alike.

Change is an inherent and inevitable aspect of life, mirroring the stages of human development from infancy to old age. Just as individuals progress through various life stages, businesses also navigate through distinct phases of change, each presenting unique challenges and opportunities. Understanding these parallels can provide valuable insights into managing change effectively within the dynamic landscape of business.

### The Stages

Infancy and childhood mark the beginning of both human life and business ventures. Infants are characterized by rapid growth, exploration, and learning. Similarly, start-ups and new businesses experience a phase of exploration, experimentation, and establishing foundational elements such as vision, mission, and initial market positioning. This stage is crucial for laying the groundwork for future development and growth. Businesses in this stage require nurturing, guidance, and strategic decision-making to ensure survival and progression.

Adolescence and puberty represent a period of significant transformation and growth in human development. It is a time marked by increased independence, identity formation, and exploration of capabilities and interests. In the business realm, this phase can be likened to the growth and expansion stage. Companies that have successfully navigated the infancy stage begin to scale operations, enter new markets, and diversify their product or service offerings. This phase often requires strategic planning, resource allocation, and risk management to capitalize on growth opportunities while maintaining organizational stability.

Adulthood signifies a stage of maturity, stability, and consolidation in both human life and business. Individuals in adulthood have typically established careers, families, and a sense of identity. Similarly, businesses that have transitioned through the growth phase reach a level of stability and market presence. They focus on optimizing operations, enhancing customer experiences, and sustaining profitability.

Adulthood in business involves strategies such as market differentiation, brand building, talent development, and strategic partnerships to ensure long-term success and competitiveness. The National Insurance Corporation (NIC) of Uganda stands as one of the oldest insurance companies in the country, having weathered the storms of time since its inception as an Act of Parliament. Initially, NIC's management team appointments were often politically motivated, and contracts were secured through syndication. However, the privatization of NIC marked a significant turning point, paving the way for a new era of performance-driven leadership.

Under the stewardship of Mr. Anthony Wyse Lubandi, NIC has undergone a remarkable transformation, shifting from a politically influenced entity to one driven by performance and strategy in a highly competitive environment. This change is not only vital but also reflects a newfound maturity and resilience in the business landscape.

NIC has strategically differentiated itself in the competitive insurance market by tailoring its products to meet diverse customer needs. The introduction of innovative insurance solutions, including customized corporate packages, health insurance plans, and micro insurance for low-income individuals, has positioned NIC as a leader in the market. This focus on market differentiation has translated into tangible results, with NIC experiencing a notable increase in market share, capturing an impressive growth the insurance market within just two years of his tenure.

Recognizing the critical role of talent in driving growth, NIC has invested heavily in talent development under Lubandi's leadership. Training programs and capacity-building initiatives have been introduced to enhance the skills and capabilities of the workforce. As a result, employee productivity has increased greatly, contributing to NIC's overall operational efficiency and customer satisfaction.

NIC has forged strategic partnerships with international reinsurance companies and technology firms to bolster its operational capabilities. Collaborations with reinsurance partners have enhanced NIC's capacity to underwrite large risks, while partnerships with technology firms have facilitated the adoption of digital solutions. These initiatives have resulted in a reduction in claims processing time and a notable improvement in operational efficiency.

NIC has experienced a remarkable increase in revenue over the past three years, driven by the successful introduction of new insurance products and expanded market reach. The company's profitability has also seen a substantial boost, with net profits growing continuously. This improvement can be attributed to cost optimization measures and enhanced risk management practices. NIC's commitment to customer-centricity has resulted in an increase in customer satisfaction rates according to internal reports. Investments in digital platforms and customer service training have ensured prompt and personalized service delivery, fostering customer loyalty and retention. We have seen NIC's success in attracting a diverse clientele and effectively competing in the insurance industry.

The transformation of the National Insurance Corporation (NIC) of Uganda under the leadership of Mr. Anthony Wyse Lubandi is a testament to the power of performance-driven leadership and strategic innovation. From its humble beginnings as a politically influenced entity, NIC has evolved into a dynamic and competitive player in the insurance industry. With a renewed focus on market differentiation, talent development, strategic partnerships, and customer- centricity, NIC is poised for continued success and growth in the years to come.

Menopause and old age in human development represent stages of transition and adaptation to changing capabilities and roles.

Similarly, businesses experience periods of transformation and evolution as markets, technologies, and consumer preferences shift. Companies in this stage may face challenges such as market saturation, disruptive innovations, or changing regulatory landscapes. Successful businesses embrace change by fostering a culture of innovation, continuous learning, and adaptability.

They reinvent themselves, explore new opportunities, and diversify revenue streams to remain relevant and resilient in a constantly evolving business environment. Old age in human development represents a phase of life characterized by wisdom, experience, and a gradual decline in physical capabilities. Similarly, in the business world, there comes a stage where companies may experience a plateau or decline in growth due to various factors such as market saturation, technological obsolescence, or changes in consumer preferences. This stage can be synonymous with the decline phase in the business life cycle.

During old age, individuals often reflect on their life achievements, consider legacy-building, and may transition into more advisory or mentoring roles. In a business context, companies in the mature or declining stage may focus on legacy preservation, cost optimization, and strategic divestments or mergers to sustain operations or gracefully exit certain markets. It's a phase that requires careful management of resources, strategic decision-making, and a realistic assessment of market positioning and competitiveness.

Successful navigation through the old age stage in business involves adaptation, innovation, and sometimes reinvention. Established companies may explore avenues such as diversification into new markets or industries, embracing digital transformations, or investing in sustainable practices to rejuvenate their brand and relevance. Moreover, partnerships or collaborations with younger, innovative start-ups can inject fresh perspectives and technologies into older businesses, fostering resilience and adaptability.

The American Motors Corporation (AMC) was a major player in the American automotive landscape during the mid-20th century, known for producing popular models such as the AMC Gremlin, Javelin, and the iconic Jeep brand. However, AMC's failure to adapt to changing market trends and competitive pressures led to its eventual decline and acquisition by larger automakers. During the 1970s and 1980s, the automotive industry experienced significant shifts, including increased competition from foreign automakers, changing consumer preferences towards smaller and more fuel-efficient vehicles, and evolving safety and emission standards. AMC struggled to keep pace with these changes due to various factors, including limited financial resources compared to larger rivals like Ford, General Motors (GM), and Chrysler.

One critical misstep was AMC's delayed entry into the compact and subcompact car segments, which gained popularity during the fuel crisis of the 1970s. While other automakers were introducing fuel- efficient models, AMC's line-up remained focused on larger vehicles, leading to a loss of market share and profitability. Additionally, the company faced challenges with outdated manufacturing facilities and a lack of innovative product development compared to competitors.

By the late 1980s, AMC's financial difficulties became more pronounced, and the company was unable to sustain operations independently. In 1987, Chrysler Corporation acquired AMC, primarily for the Jeep brand, while discontinuing most of AMC's other vehicle lines.

This example highlights the importance of agility, foresight, and adaptability in the automotive industry. AMC's failure to anticipate and respond effectively to changing market dynamics and consumer preferences ultimately led to its decline and acquisition by a larger competitor, underscoring the need for continuous innovation and strategic planning to remain competitive in the fast-paced automotive sector.

Conversely, the stages of human development relate closely to the phases of change in business, from infancy to old age. Each stage brings unique challenges and opportunities, requiring strategic planning, adaptability, and resilience. By understanding these parallels, businesses can navigate change effectively, capitalize on growth opportunities, and sustain long-term success in an ever-changing world.

**Dynamic Nature of Change**
Change is inherent in the fabric of life, constantly reshaping circumstances, perspectives, and opportunities. For humans, change manifests as personal growth, learning experiences, career transitions, and evolving life stages. Embracing change allows individuals to break free from their comfort zones, explore new horizons, discover strengths and weaknesses, and unlock their full potential. In business, change is a cornerstone of organizational evolution, driving strategies, market responsiveness, product innovations, and competitive edge. Businesses that embrace change proactively anticipate market shifts, technological advancements, and consumer trends, positioning themselves for relevance and sustainability.

**Adaptation and Resilience**
Change fosters adaptation and resilience, empowering individuals and businesses to navigate challenges, setbacks, and uncertainties effectively. Human resilience is demonstrated through coping mechanisms, problem-solving skills, emotional intelligence, and the ability to bounce back from adversity stronger and wiser. Similarly, businesses that prioritize adaptability and resilience thrive

in dynamic environments, leveraging change as an opportunity to pivot strategies, optimize operations, and seize emerging opportunities. Adaptable businesses anticipate change, embrace innovation, and leverage their strengths to stay ahead in competitive markets.

### Innovation and Creativity

Change fuels innovation and creativity, unleashing new ideas, solutions, and possibilities. Human creativity flourishes in environments that encourage experimentation, open-mindedness, and diverse perspectives. Change prompts individuals to think outside the box, challenge norms, and explore unconventional paths, leading to breakthroughs in science, technology, arts, and entrepreneurship. In businesses, a culture that embraces change fosters a spirit of innovation, collaboration, and risk-taking. Innovative businesses disrupt industries, create value for customers, and pioneer transformative solutions that address evolving needs and preferences.

### Continuous Improvement

Change is synonymous with continuous improvement, driving individuals and businesses to strive for excellence, efficiency, and effectiveness. Humans embrace change as a catalyst for personal development, setting goals, acquiring new skills, and seeking feedback for ongoing growth. Likewise, businesses that prioritize continuous improvement processes such as Lean Management, Six Sigma, or Agile methodologies enhance operational excellence, quality standards, and customer satisfaction. Continuous improvement initiatives optimize processes, reduce waste, and foster a culture of excellence and innovation within organizations.

## Advent of Opportunities

Change brings forth opportunities for exploration, expansion, and transformation. Human beings seize opportunities presented by change to explore new careers, embark on entrepreneurial ventures, pursue educational endeavours, or engage in meaningful experiences that enrich their lives. When it comes to business, change creates opportunities for market expansion, strategic partnerships, digital transformation, and disruptive innovation. Businesses that embrace change proactively identify and capitalize on opportunities, positioning themselves for sustainable growth and long-term success.

There are notable figures in history, who demonstrated exceptional leadership by transforming successful organizations in Europe, shifting their focus and strategies to achieve even greater success in different industries. These stories showcase visionary leadership, strategic innovation, and the ability to adapt to changing landscapes, contributing significantly to the economic and entrepreneurial landscapes of their respective countries.

## Thor Bjørklund – From Sawmill to Cheese Slicer Empire

Thor Bjørklund, a Norwegian entrepreneur, is renowned for his transformative journey from the timber industry to creating one of Norway's most iconic household products—the cheese slicer.

In the early 1920s, Bjørklund was involved in the timber business, operating a sawmill in Lillehammer.

However, he recognized an opportunity for innovation and diversification in the kitchenware market. Drawing inspiration from a carpenter's plane, Bjørklund designed and patented the first-ever cheese slicer in 1925, revolutionizing the way people prepared and served cheese. His cheese slicer design was simple yet effective, gaining popularity among households and catering businesses across Norway and beyond. Bjørklund's entrepreneurial vision and shift from the timber industry to kitchen utensils not only transformed his own business but also contributed to Norway's reputation for design innovation and quality craftsmanship in consumer goods.

**Mikhail Khodorkovsky – From Oil to Philanthropy**
Mikhail Khodorkovsky, a prominent Russian businessman, rose to prominence in the 1990s as the founder of Yukos, one of Russia's largest oil companies. Under his leadership, Yukos became a major player in the Russian energy sector, achieving substantial success and profitability. However, Khodorkovsky's entrepreneurial journey took a significant turn that went beyond business success. In the early 2000s, Khodorkovsky shifted his focus from purely business endeavours to philanthropic and social initiatives aimed at promoting education, civil society development, and human rights in Russia. He founded the Open Russia Foundation, a non-profit organization dedicated to supporting democracy, transparency, and civic engagement.

Khodorkovsky's transition from the oil industry to philanthropy showcased a profound commitment to social responsibility and positive impact beyond traditional business realms. Despite facing political challenges and legal controversies, his advocacy for social change and democratic values remains a notable aspect of his legacy. These historical business figures relay to us, the transformative power of visionary leadership, strategic pivots, and the pursuit of broader societal impact.

Their journeys highlight key lessons for modern

entrepreneurs and business leaders:
*Recognizing Opportunities Amidst Change:* Successful leaders are adept at recognizing emerging opportunities, whether in product innovation (as seen with Thor Bjørklund) or social impact initiatives (as demonstrated by Mikhail Khodorkovsky).
*Adaptability and Diversification to Change:* The ability to pivot and diversify business interests based on market dynamics and strategic goals is crucial for sustained success and relevance.
*Social Responsibility in Change Management:* Beyond financial success, leaders can make meaningful contributions to society by championing ethical practices, corporate social responsibility, and philanthropic endeavours.
*Legacy Building in Change:* Transformative leaders leave a lasting legacy not only through business achievements but also through their contributions to industry innovation, societal progress, and positive change.

These stories of historical business figures serve as inspiration for current and future generations of entrepreneurs and leaders, showcasing the transformative potential of visionary thinking, strategic adaptation, and a commitment to broader values and impact beyond traditional business metrics.

Change is a dynamic and positive element that drives personal growth, organizational resilience, innovation, and opportunities in both human lives and business environments. Embracing change as a vital principle empowers individuals and businesses to adapt, evolve, and thrive in an ever-changing world, unlocking potential, fostering creativity, and driving positive transformations that contribute to individual fulfilment and business success.

# 14.

## Code, Image and Brand

Image and brand are crucial aspects of both human families and businesses, influencing how they are perceived by others and their overall success. Mishandling image or code of conduct has historically led to catastrophic incidents. In a family setting, image is closely tied to reputation and how the family is viewed by society. For instance, in Ireland, where family ties and community reputation hold significant importance, a family's image can be tarnished by scandals or improper behaviour. One such scenario could involve a prominent family member being involved in a public scandal, causing embarrassment and damaging the family's standing in the community.

Similarly, businesses have their own image, often referred to as their brand. A brand encompasses not just the products or services offered but also the values, reputation, and overall perception by customers and stakeholders. In Spain, where businesses often have deep-rooted traditions and values, a company's brand can be severely impacted by ethical lapses or controversies. For example, a company found to have exploited workers or engaged in unethical practices may face boycotts, legal repercussions, and a damaged reputation that takes years to rebuild.

Founded in 1864, Vega Sicilia is one of Spain's most renowned and prestigious wineries, known for producing high-quality wines with a focus on tradition and excellence. Throughout its history, Vega Sicilia has been owned and operated by the Álvarez family, who have upheld a commitment to preserving the estate's heritage and legacy. The family's dedication to quality winemaking and their respect for the land have been central to the company's identity and reputation.

Vega Sicilia's wines, particularly their flagship wine "Único," have achieved international acclaim, earning recognition for their exceptional craftsmanship and unique character. Despite changes in the wine industry and market dynamics over the years, Vega Sicilia has remained steadfast in its adherence to traditional winemaking methods and uncompromising quality standards.

The company's deep-rooted family values, commitment to excellence, and unwavering dedication to producing exceptional wines have earned Vega Sicilia a reputation as one of Spain's most respected and iconic wineries. This reputation has been built over generations and serves as a testament to the enduring legacy of family-owned businesses in the wine industry. In a family, a code of conduct outlines the values, principles, and expected behaviour of its members. It sets boundaries and guides interactions within the family unit. Failure to adhere to this code can lead to conflicts, breakdowns in trust, and even estrangement.

An example could be a family member involved in fraudulent activities, causing not only legal troubles but also emotional distress within the family. Similarly, businesses have codes of conduct or ethics that define acceptable behaviours and practices within the organization. These codes often cover areas such as honesty, integrity, respect for others, and compliance with laws and regulations. Violations of these codes can have severe consequences, both internally and externally. For instance, a company in Ireland known for its ethical practices and transparency could face public outrage and legal actions if it's revealed that they were involved in environmental pollution or corruption.

The Steinhoff International scandal originated in South Africa but had implications for various countries including Austria. Steinhoff International was a multinational retail holding company, and its founder, Markus Jooste, was a prominent figure in the business world. In December 2017, Steinhoff announced that it was investigating accounting irregularities, and soon after, Markus Jooste resigned as CEO amidst allegations of financial misconduct. This scandal led to a massive decline in Steinhoff's stock value, causing significant financial losses for investors and creditors globally.

The fallout from this scandal affected various subsidiaries and stakeholders, including Austria-based Kika/Leiner, a furniture retail chain owned by Steinhoff. Kika/Leiner faced financial difficulties and restructuring due to its ties with Steinhoff. Particular issues within a family business can have far-reaching consequences.

In both family and business contexts, mishandling images or code of conduct can lead to catastrophic incidents. These incidents can range from financial losses and legal troubles to irreparable damage to relationships and reputations. Therefore, it's crucial for both families and businesses to prioritize their image, brand, and adherence to ethical standards to ensure long-term success and positive societal impact.

# 15.

# Reproduction

The analogy between the cycle of life and the growth and expansion of businesses through franchising, partnerships, and expansion into new markets is a compelling reflection of the interconnectedness between human endeavours and corporate strategies. This phenomenon mirrors the innate drive for growth, evolution, and creating a lasting legacy, shared by both individuals and businesses. Franchising has been a powerful strategy for businesses to reproduce and expand their reach. Ray Kroc, the visionary behind McDonald's global success, famously stated, "The two most important requirements for major success are: first, being in the right place at the right time, and second, doing something about it."

Ray Kroc knew that his product served the average person and that the average person was everywhere. He knew that the right place was everywhere and he wanted to be there when everyone is there. This is seen in Mc Donald's unique business hours. They work several shifts a day to keep it available. He had a keen understanding of catering to the average person's needs and leveraging the ubiquity of his product. His vision was to make McDonald's accessible and available to everyone, everywhere, and at any time they craved it. This is reflected in McDonald's unique business hours and multiple shifts, ensuring customers can enjoy their offerings throughout the day.

"We provide food that customers love, day after day, year after year. People just want more of it", said Ray. McDonald's replicated its successful business model across the globe, allowing local entrepreneurs to operate under the McDonald's brand while adhering to standardized processes and quality control. This approach not only facilitated rapid expansion but also enabled McDonald's to cater to diverse markets and consumer preferences while maintaining a consistent brand identity.

The concept of reproduction is one of the most profound elements of humanity and we see it constantly manifested in businesses for growth and expansion as human communities would.

This is the humanity of Business!

Furthermore, expanding into new markets is a fundamental strategy for businesses seeking growth and global presence. Coca-Cola, a company with a rich history and global footprint, exemplifies this approach. As former CEO Neville Isdell remarked, "We need to develop the habit of reinventing ourselves." Coca-Cola expanded beyond its core beverage offerings into diverse markets, adapting its products to local tastes and preferences while maintaining a strong brand identity.

The expansion into emerging economies like China and India has been instrumental in sustaining Coca-Cola's growth trajectory and reinforcing its position as a leading beverage company worldwide. This expansion not only generates revenue but also creates employment opportunities, fosters economic development, and contributes to local communities— a testament to the broader impact businesses can have on society.

The growth and expansion of businesses through

franchising, partnerships, and global expansion reflect the dynamic nature of entrepreneurship and the quest for enduring success. By drawing insights from key business figures and real-life examples, we can appreciate the strategic acumen, collaborative spirit, and transformative potential inherent in business endeavours, paralleling the aspirations and impact of human endeavours on a broader scale.

# 16.

## Posterity and Succession

Posterity and succession are profound concepts that hold significant importance in both the realms of humans and businesses. These concepts not only reflect the passage of time and the continuity of existence but also underscore the interconnectedness between generations and the strategies for sustainable growth and legacy building.

In the context of humans, posterity refers to future generations, descendants, and the enduring impact of individuals on society and culture. It encompasses the idea of leaving a meaningful legacy, passing on knowledge, values, and traditions, and contributing to the betterment of future generations.

Posterity is closely linked to concepts such as family lineage, heritage, and the collective memory of communities. Succession, in human terms, refers to the transfer of roles, responsibilities, and assets from one generation to the next, ensuring continuity, leadership transitions, and the preservation of familial or organizational legacies. Similarly, in the realm of businesses, posterity and succession play crucial roles in shaping the long-term sustainability, growth, and resilience of enterprises. Posterity for businesses involves strategic planning, innovation, and investment in initiatives that secure the organization's future relevance, competitive advantage, and positive impact on stakeholders and society. It encompasses considerations such as organizational culture, values, brand reputation, and corporate social responsibility efforts that contribute to long-term success and legacy building.

Succession planning in businesses is a structured approach to managing leadership transitions, talent development, and knowledge transfer within an organization. It involves identifying and grooming future leaders, creating pathways for career progression, and ensuring a smooth transition of key roles and responsibilities. Effective succession planning mitigates risks associated with leadership gaps, loss of institutional knowledge, and disruptions to business operations, thereby safeguarding continuity and organizational resilience.

The parallels between humans and businesses regarding posterity and succession reveal several insightful perspectives:

### Legacy

Both humans and businesses aspire to leave a positive legacy that outlasts their immediate presence. Humans may focus on family values, cultural heritage, philanthropic contributions, or intellectual achievements, while businesses aim to establish a lasting impact through innovation, ethical business practices, and corporate citizenship initiatives.

In Mauritius, several businesses have demonstrated a commitment to leaving a positive legacy that extends beyond their immediate presence. Terra, formerly known as Terra Mauricia Ltd offers vital references. Terra is a leading sugar producer in Mauritius that has transformed its operations to focus on sustainable agriculture and environmental stewardship. Terra has implemented various initiatives aimed at reducing its environmental impact and promoting sustainable development. For example, the company has diversified its agricultural activities beyond traditional sugarcane cultivation to include renewable energy production, organic farming, and agro-tourism.

Additionally, the group has invested in eco-friendly technologies such as drip irrigation systems and integrated pest management practices to minimize water usage and chemical inputs in its agricultural operations. The company also engages in community development projects, including educational programs, healthcare initiatives, and infrastructure improvements in rural areas.

Terra's commitment to sustainability and community development demonstrates its dedication to leaving a positive legacy for future generations in Mauritius.

Medine Sugar Estates is another notable reference. Originally focused on sugar production, Medine has diversified its business activities to include real estate development, hospitality, energy, and leisure. In recent years, Medine has placed a strong emphasis on sustainability and environmental conservation. The company has implemented various initiatives to reduce its environmental footprint, such as investing in renewable energy sources like solar power and biomass. Medine has also adopted sustainable agricultural practices, including organic farming and water conservation measures.

Medine is also actively involved in community development projects aimed at improving the well- being of local residents. These initiatives include education and vocational training programs, healthcare services, and infrastructure development in neighbouring communities. By embracing sustainable practices and contributing to the social and economic development of Mauritius, Medine Sugar Estates is positioning itself to leave a positive legacy for future generations as well as secure their relevance.

### Knowledge Transfer

Both domains recognize the importance of passing on knowledge, skills, and experiences to future generations or successors. In families, this may involve teaching traditions, values, and practical skills. In businesses, it includes mentorship programs, training initiatives, and knowledge management strategies to ensure continuity of expertise and organizational learning.

The transition of power in ancient Rome from Julius Caesar to Augustus showcases both the challenges and opportunities of succession. Augustus' leadership and reforms set the stage for the Pax Romana, a period of relative peace and stability.

Microsoft's succession from Bill Gates to Steve Ballmer and then to Satya Nadella illustrates effective leadership transition in a tech giant. Satya Nadella's focus on cloud computing and cultural transformation has propelled Microsoft's growth and innovation in the 21st century.

### Leadership Transition

Succession planning is critical for seamless leadership transitions in both human and business contexts. Families and businesses alike invest in identifying and developing potential leaders, providing opportunities for growth and development, and creating clear pathways for succession to maintain stability and effectiveness.

In 2001, Geoff Dixon took over as CEO of Qantas Airways during a challenging period marked by industry turbulence, economic downturns, and increased competition. Under Dixon's leadership, Qantas implemented strategic measures such as cost-cutting initiatives, fleet modernization, and international expansion, which helped the airline navigate through turbulent times and maintain its market position.

In 2008, Alan Joyce succeeded Geoff Dixon as CEO of Qantas. Joyce faced various challenges, including global financial crises, rising fuel costs, and labor disputes. However, his leadership style, emphasis on operational efficiency, and strategic decisions like launching the low-cost carrier Jetstar and forming alliances with international airlines contributed to Qantas' resilience and growth.

More often than not, businesses must be prepared to adapt to new leadership styles, strategies, and market conditions. Effective succession planning, continuity in vision, and the ability to address challenges with innovation and resilience are critical elements that ensure successful leadership transitions in both human and business contexts.

### Adaptability and Innovation

Both humans and businesses must adapt to changing environments and embrace innovation to thrive in the long term. Whether it's adapting to new technologies, evolving market trends, or societal shifts, the ability to innovate and stay relevant is key to sustained success and resilience.

Marie Curie's ground-breaking research on radioactivity not only earned her Nobel Prizes in Physics and Chemistry but also paved the way for advancements in medical diagnostics and treatment.

Toyota's renowned production system, developed by Taiichi Ohno, revolutionized the automotive industry by emphasizing continuous improvement, waste reduction, and employee empowerment. This approach has been widely adopted across industries globally.

Over to Tanzania in East Africa, the leadership transition at CRDB Bank from Dr. Charles Kimei to Abdulmajid

Nsekela stands as a remarkable example of effective succession in Tanzania, leading to significant growth and innovation. Dr. Charles Kimei's tenure as CEO of CRDB Bank began in 1998 and lasted two decades. Under his leadership, CRDB Bank evolved into one of Tanzania's foremost financial institutions. Dr. Kimei was instrumental in driving robust financial performance, expanding the branch network, and introducing innovative banking solutions. His strategic vision and leadership laid a solid foundation for the bank's success.

In 2018, Dr. Kimei retired, and Abdulmajid Nsekela, an experienced banker with a strong track record in the industry, took over as CEO. This transition was not just a change in leadership but a strategic move to propel CRDB Bank into a new era of growth and modernization. Under Nsekela's leadership, CRDB Bank has reached new heights. His tenure has been marked by a strong focus on digital transformation, significantly enhancing the bank's technological capabilities. Nsekela has driven the development of mobile banking, internet banking, and other digital platforms, making banking services more accessible to the Tanzanian population. Moreover, Nsekela has placed a significant emphasis on financial inclusion, working to bring more unbanked and underbanked populations into the formal banking system. This strategy has not only contributed to CRDB Bank's growth but has also supported broader economic development in Tanzania.

The financial performance of CRDB Bank under Nsekela has been impressive, with the bank showing increasing profits and expanding its market share. His leadership has ensured that CRDB Bank continues to be a leader in innovation and customer service in the Tanzanian banking sector. The transition from Dr. Charles Kimei to Abdulmajid Nsekela at CRDB Bank is a prime example of how effective leadership succession can drive a company to new levels of growth and innovation. This case highlights the importance of strategic planning in leadership transitions and the impact of visionary leadership on a company's success.

### Values and Ethics

Posterity and succession planning are rooted in core values and ethical considerations. Humans pass down values such as integrity, compassion, and resilience to future generations, while businesses uphold ethical standards, corporate governance principles, and sustainability practices that reflect their values and contribute to long-term success.

Mahatma Gandhi's nonviolent resistance during India's independence movement exemplifies the power of values such as truth, nonviolence, and social justice in driving significant societal change.
Patagonia, an American outdoor clothing company, is known for its commitment to environmental sustainability and ethical business practices. Their initiatives, such as the "Worn Wear" program promoting product durability and repair, align with their values and resonate with environmentally conscious consumers.

### Long-Term Sustainability

Both individuals and businesses are concerned with long-term sustainability and well-being. Humans may focus on environmental stewardship, social justice, and community engagement for a sustainable future, while businesses integrate sustainability into their strategies, operations, and supply chains to minimize environmental impact and create shared value. The Green Revolution led by Norman Borlaug in the mid-20th century transformed agricultural practices, significantly increasing food production and addressing global hunger challenges.

Unilever, a multinational consumer goods company, has embraced sustainability through initiatives like the Sustainable Living Plan. They prioritize environmental footprint reduction, social impact, and sustainable sourcing across their product portfolio. Each historical occurrence reiterates the interconnectedness of personal and organizational legacies, the importance of strategic planning and adaptation for long-term sustainability, and the role of values, ethics, and innovation in shaping a positive impact on future generations.

By recognizing and leveraging these parallels, individuals and businesses can align their actions and strategies to create enduring value, contribute to positive social change, and build a legacy that transcends time. The enduring impact of visionary leadership, the importance of values-driven decisions, and the role of innovation and sustainability continues to shape a better future for generations to come.

# 17.

## Death

Death, a concept often associated with human mortality, finds a parallel in the realm of businesses, reflecting profound similarities and poignant contrasts between the two domains. Both businesses and humans undergo life cycles characterized by growth, maturity, and eventual decline or transformation, showcasing the cyclical nature of existence. At the core of this comparison lies the inevitability of change and transformation. Just as humans experience various stages of life, from birth to ageing and eventually passing away, businesses too traverse a similar path. A start-up emerges with an idea, fuelled by enthusiasm and innovation akin to a newborn's vitality. As it matures, it faces challenges, adapts to market demands, and strives to establish a sustainable presence, mirroring the journey of human development and learning.

However, the most significant parallel between death in human life and businesses is the concept of endings and new beginnings. When a business fails or faces obsolescence, it can be seen as a form of 'death' in the corporate world. Yet, this ending often paves the way for new opportunities, innovations, and the birth of new ventures. Similarly, in human life, death is not merely an end but a transition, symbolizing the continuity of life through generations.

The impact of death in both contexts extends beyond

the individual or business entity to their ecosystem. Just as the passing of a person affects their family, friends, and community, the closure or transformation of a business influences its employees, stakeholders, and the broader economic landscape. This ripple effect underscores the interconnectedness and interdependence inherent in life and business dynamics.

The early 2000s witnessed the dramatic collapse of Alborz Insurance, one of Iran's largest insurance companies. This event not only devastated the company itself but also sent shockwaves through the Iranian economy, demonstrating the interconnectedness and interdependence inherent in business and economic dynamics. The downfall of Alborz Insurance had far-reaching effects, impacting employees, policyholders, the insurance sector, the financial system, and the broader economic landscape.

The collapse of Alborz Insurance resulted in significant job losses. At its peak, the company employed over 1,000 individuals across various departments, including sales, claims, underwriting, and administrative roles. The company's insolvency led to the immediate termination of these jobs, directly affecting the livelihoods of the employees and their families. This loss of employment created a ripple effect of economic hardship and uncertainty, contributing to increased financial strain for many households.

The collapse of Alborz Insurance severely undermined public confidence in the Iranian insurance sector. Several indicators reflected this loss of trust. Firstly, there was a marked decrease in new policy sales across the industry. Individuals and businesses, wary of experiencing similar outcomes, were hesitant to purchase insurance from other companies. Additionally, many existing policyholders began to withdraw or cancel their policies, exacerbating liquidity issues for other insurers.

Media coverage and public discourse further highlighted the crisis. Prominent newspapers such as the "Tehran Times" and "Financial Tribune" extensively covered the collapse, emphasizing the failures in regulatory oversight and the resulting lack of trust in the insurance sector. These reports and articles underscored systemic issues and contributed to a broader sense of scepticism towards the industry.

The bankruptcy of Alborz Insurance had profound implications for the Iranian financial system. The company's failure to meet its financial obligations created a domino effect on creditors and associated financial institutions. Banks that had extended loans to Alborz Insurance were forced to write off substantial amounts, impacting their balance sheets and reducing their lending capacity. This tightening of credit conditions affected other businesses and individuals, leading to a broader economic slowdown.

The collapse also led to increased regulatory scrutiny. The Central Insurance of Iran (CII) implemented more rigorous auditing and capital requirements for insurance companies. While these measures were intended to restore confidence, they also increased operational costs for insurers, some of whom struggled to comply with the new regulations. The heightened regulatory environment aimed to prevent similar collapses but also revealed the fragility within the sector.

In the long term, the collapse of Alborz Insurance prompted significant changes within the Iranian insurance industry. The immediate aftermath saw market consolidation, with smaller and weaker insurance companies either going out of business or being acquired by larger, more stable entities. This consolidation aimed to create a more resilient industry capable of withstanding financial shocks.

The industry also underwent a push towards modernization and reform. Improved risk management practices, enhanced corporate governance, and greater transparency were introduced to rebuild trust among policyholders and investors. Additionally, the government implemented new consumer protection measures to safeguard the interests of policyholders, ensuring that insurance companies could not easily default on their obligations.

The failure of a single, large entity can have extensive and lasting impacts on the broader economy. The immediate job losses, loss of confidence in the insurance sector, and the ripple effects on the financial system and regulatory environment highlight the interconnected nature of economic dynamics. It Is also important to maintain robust financial oversight, strong institutional resilience, and the need for continuous reform to maintain public confidence in key economic sectors.

Furthermore, the manner in which individuals and businesses approach death or endings reflects their resilience, adaptability, and capacity for renewal. Those who embrace change, learn from setbacks, and envision new beginnings are better equipped to navigate the inevitable cycles of life or market fluctuations. This adaptability is a hallmark of survival and growth, fostering resilience in the face of adversity. However, it's crucial to note that while the analogy between death and business cycles provides insights into their dynamics, there are fundamental differences. Unlike human life, businesses can undergo 'rebirth' through restructuring, rebranding, or reinvention, highlighting the malleability of corporate entities compared to biological life forms.

The comparison of death in relation to businesses and humans reveals profound parallels in life cycles, transformations, and resilience. By acknowledging these similarities, individuals and businesses can cultivate a deeper understanding of impermanence, embrace change proactively, and harness the power of renewal to thrive in dynamic environments.

Despite their best efforts, not all businesses will survive in the long run. Some may face insurmountable challenges and ultimately "die" by being de-registered or going out of business. However, this doesn't have to be the end.

### Business Life Expectancy

In the world of business, not every venture is destined for success. Despite the best efforts of entrepreneurs and business owners, some companies simply cannot weather the storm and ultimately meet their demise. Businesses in Africa often face a challenging landscape marked by limited access to capital, infrastructure gaps, and regulatory complexities. These factors can contribute to a relatively lower life expectancy for businesses in the region compared to more developed economies.

However, African businesses showcase resilience and innovation, akin to the hardy acacia trees of the savannah, adapting to challenges and leveraging opportunities to carve out sustainable niches in diverse sectors. Start-ups and businesses in Africa often face challenges that can impact their longevity. On average, start-ups in Africa may have a shorter life expectancy compared to more developed regions, with some studies suggesting that around 50% of start-ups in Africa do not survive beyond the first five years of operation.

In Europe, businesses benefit from a more stable and established ecosystem with access to capital, developed infrastructure, and a supportive regulatory environment. This conducive environment often leads to a longer life expectancy for businesses, resembling trees in a temperate forest that thrive in a nurturing and stable habitat. Established networks, strong consumer bases, and a culture of innovation contribute to the longevity and success of businesses in Europe. The business environment in Europe is relatively stable and supportive, leading to longer life expectancies for start-ups and businesses. On average, start-ups in Europe have a higher survival rate, with around 70% to 80% of start-ups surviving beyond the first five years.

Asia represents a dynamic and rapidly evolving business landscape, akin to a bustling rainforest teeming with opportunities and challenges. Businesses in Asia experience rapid growth, intense competition, and diverse market dynamics. This environment fosters both innovation and disruption, with businesses navigating complex ecosystems to sustain their competitiveness and longevity. Strategic agility, market insights, and adaptability are key factors that influence the life expectancy of businesses in Asia. Asia is known for its dynamic and competitive business landscape. Start-ups in Asia often experience rapid growth but also face intense competition and market dynamics. On average, start-ups in Asia have a moderate life expectancy, with approximately 60% to 70% of start-ups surviving beyond the first five years.

In America, particularly in the United States, businesses operate in a vibrant and diverse economic ecosystem resembling a mixed woodland. This ecosystem encompasses established industry leaders, disruptive start-ups, and a robust venture capital landscape. While American businesses benefit from a culture of entrepreneurship, access to capital, and technological advancements, they also face challenges such as market saturation, regulatory shifts, and global economic dynamics.

Successful businesses in America exhibit resilience, innovation, and strategic vision, factors that contribute to their extended life expectancy and impact in the global marketplace. Particularly in the United States, start-ups benefit from a robust ecosystem of venture capital, innovation hubs, and entrepreneurial culture. This contributes to a relatively higher life expectancy for start-ups compared to many other regions. On average, around 70% to 80% of start-ups in the United States survive beyond the first five years.

While the life expectancy of businesses in Africa can be uncertain, there are valuable lessons to be learned from the failures of those that have come before. Entrepreneurs and business owners can gain insights into the common pitfalls that can lead to business failure and take proactive steps to avoid them. Remember, the end of one business does not have to be the end of your entrepreneurial journey – learn from the mistakes of others and use that knowledge to build a stronger, more resilient business for the future.

# 18.

# Resurrection

The ability of businesses to "resurrect" by reinventing themselves, exploring new opportunities, and adapting to a changing world is a testament to their resilience and capacity for transformation. History is replete with examples of businesses that faced challenges or near-failure but managed to stage impressive comebacks through strategic pivots, innovative thinking, and a strong focus on customer needs.

**MTN Uganda**
MTN Uganda provides a compelling example of a business that has experienced significant resurgence and transformation. In the early 2000s, MTN Uganda faced stiff competition from other telecommunications providers, and its market share was under pressure. The company's financial performance was also challenged by the broader economic environment and regulatory changes.

However, MTN Uganda embarked on a strategic transformation under new leadership. MTN invested heavily in expanding its network coverage across the country, ensuring that even remote areas had access to reliable mobile services. The introduction of mobile money services, particularly the MTN Mobile Money platform, revolutionized the way Ugandans conducted financial transactions. This service became a critical driver of financial inclusion, allowing people to send and receive money, pay bills, and conduct other financial activities via their mobile phones.

MTN Uganda focused on enhancing customer experience through improved service delivery, customer support, and innovative marketing campaigns. This helped to rebuild customer trust and loyalty. They formed strategic partnerships with banks, utility companies, and other businesses which enabled MTN to offer a wide range of services and applications to its customers, further embedding itself in the daily lives of Ugandans.

As a result of these efforts, MTN Uganda not only regained its market position but also became a dominant player in the telecommunications sector. The company's resurgence has had a positive impact on the broader economy by enhancing connectivity, promoting financial inclusion, and fostering innovation.

### Equity Bank Kenya

Equity Bank Kenya is another illustrative case of remarkable business transformation and resurgence. In the early 2000s, Equity Bank was a struggling building society on the brink of collapse, with significant financial woes and a limited customer base. The turnaround began under the visionary leadership of Dr. James Mwangi, who implemented a series of strategic changes that revitalized the bank: Equity Bank shifted its focus towards serving the unbanked and underbanked populations. By offering accessible banking services to low-income individuals, small businesses, and rural communities, the bank tapped into a vast, underserved market.

In the early days of Equity Bank's transformation in Kenya, banking was an exclusive affair. Customers were required to dress formally to be admitted, and security measures included pat-downs at the entrance. Additionally, those bringing in money that smelled of fish or pineapples—a common issue for market traders—were often turned away.

Recognizing the untapped potential in the low-income segment, Dr. James Mwangi, introduced the "Jijenge Savings Account." This account, whose name translated from Swahili means "let's build ourselves," was designed specifically for the common person. This inclusive approach resonated with the unbanked and underbanked, leading to a surge in new account sign-ups from low-income individuals and high-turnover small businesses.

The Jijenge Savings Account played a pivotal role in transforming Equity Bank into the "people's bank." Today, Equity Bank is renowned for its commitment to financial inclusion and remains a leading financial institution in Kenya. The introduction of mobile banking services, such as Equitel, and agent banking networks significantly increased the bank's reach. Customers could now access banking services through their mobile phones and local agents, making banking more convenient and accessible.

Equity Bank emphasized financial literacy and customer education, empowering clients to make informed financial decisions. This approach built trust and loyalty among customers. The bank formed strategic partnerships with international organizations, investors, and development partners, which provided the necessary capital and support for its expansion. Additionally, Equity Bank diversified its services to include insurance, investment banking, and other financial services. Investment in cutting-edge technology and innovative banking solutions ensured that Equity Bank remained competitive in the rapidly evolving financial services industry.

These strategic initiatives transformed Equity Bank from

a struggling institution into one of Kenya's leading banks. Today, Equity Bank is renowned for its extensive branch network, innovative services, and significant role in promoting financial inclusion and economic development in Kenya and beyond.

In the 1970s and 1980s, Japanese automakers like Toyota faced scepticism and challenges in the American market. However, Toyota's focus on quality, efficiency, and innovation, epitomized by the Toyota Production System and the introduction of fuel- efficient vehicles like the Prius, helped it gain a significant foothold. Today, Toyota is a global automotive powerhouse known for its reliability and sustainability efforts.

These are all depictions of the resilience and adaptability of businesses in navigating challenges and seizing new opportunities. Whether through technological innovation, strategic partnerships, diversification, or customer-centric approaches, successful businesses demonstrate a willingness to evolve and reinvent themselves to thrive in a dynamic and competitive landscape. The ability of businesses to "resurrect" through reinvention and adaptation underscores the importance of agility, vision, and strategic foresight. By learning from past successes and failures, businesses can position themselves for sustained growth and relevance, even in the face of disruptive forces and market uncertainties.

# 19.

## Soul and Spirit

The concept of a soul is deeply rooted in various philosophical, religious, and spiritual beliefs. In general terms, a soul is often described as the immaterial essence or spirit that is believed to exist within a living being, separate from the physical body. Different belief systems have different interpretations of the soul, ranging from it being the seat of emotions, consciousness, and identity to being eternal and existing beyond physical death.

**The Soul of Business**
The concept of the "soul of a business" Is a metaphorical way of describing the essence or core identity of a company. It encompasses the values, principles, culture, and mission that define the company beyond just its tangible assets or operations. Just as humans have a unique identity and purpose, businesses also have a distinct "soul" that guides their decisions, actions, and relationships within their ecosystem.

This notion is often emphasized in discussions about corporate culture, vision statements, and ethical practices. The soul of a business reflects its character, beliefs, and aspirations, shaping how it interacts with employees, customers, and society at large. Businesses with a strong and authentic soul tend to have a clearer sense of purpose, stronger employee engagement, and better alignment with their stakeholders' expectations.

Let us journey to the Netherlands, at Tony's Chocolonely for reference. This company was founded in 2005 with a mission to produce and sell chocolate that is 100% slave-free. Their goal is not only to create delicious chocolate but also to address the issue of child labor and modern slavery in the cocoa industry. Tony's Chocolonely's soul is deeply rooted in their core values of fairness, transparency, and social responsibility. They actively work towards creating a fair and sustainable supply chain, from sourcing cocoa beans directly from partner cooperatives in Ghana and Ivory Coast to paying farmers a fair price for their work. The company's packaging and marketing also highlight its commitment to ethical practices, raising awareness among consumers about the importance of fair trade and ethical consumption.

Through their actions and advocacy, Tony's Chocolonely has not only built a successful business but also inspired other companies to prioritize social impact and sustainability in their operations. Their story serves as a compelling illustration of how a business can embody a strong soul by aligning its mission with positive social change. The essence of a business or an Individual's soul is not solely discerned through formal declarations or written values, but rather through the fundamental fabric of their conduct and decision-making processes.

Similar to human morality, where actions can vary drastically, a business's true nature is revealed through the ethical choices it makes and how it operates within its societal context. Just as individuals exhibit diverse behaviours and motivations, businesses can demonstrate varying levels of ethical consciousness and social responsibility, shaping their impact on stakeholders and communities. Understanding these complexities is essential in evaluating the genuine soul or character of a business entity.

**The Spirit of Business**
The spirit of a business encapsulates its vitality, essence, and demeanour, extending beyond its visible operations and offerings. It encompasses the intangible attributes that sculpt the company's ethos, vision, and engagements with stakeholders. Have you come across the saying "With every breath I take"? It embodies a resolute determination that resonates with one's core essence in pursuing goals. In Hebrew, the term "spirit" translates to Numa (meaning breath) or רוח (ruach), symbolizing the breath, wind, or a broader spiritual essence in Jewish heritage. Just like the intangible yet influential nature of wind or breath, a business's spirit is felt through its various facets.

Within business realms, this intangible element distinguishes an organization. It materializes through innovation, entrepreneurial drive, ethical practices, social responsibility, client focus, collaboration, and purpose. The spirit of a business shines through its capacity to innovate, adapt, and embrace advancements, staying competitive and exploring new horizons. A spirited entrepreneurial drive fosters creativity, risk-taking, and seizing opportunities. A business's spirit is evident in its commitment to ethical conduct, social accountability, and sustainability. Such values showcase integrity, responsibility, and a genuine concern for societal and environmental well-being.
Customer-centricity mirrors the spirit of understanding, delivering value, and surpassing expectations, crucial for building enduring relationships and loyalty.

A harmonious and collaborative work environment reflects the spirit of unity, teamwork, and mutual respect, enhancing creativity, productivity, and overall employee satisfaction. Ultimately, a business's spirit aligns with its overarching vision, mission, and purpose, guiding decisions and fostering a sense of purposeful alignment across the organization. In essence, the spirit of a business encompasses a harmonious blend of values, attitudes, and behaviours that define its character, culture, and broader impact within the business landscape and beyond.

## The X Factor

There is a man whose words I respect and heed above all others. I heard him say this once, "Anyone who has succeeded at anything noteworthy has bowed to an altar. There are only two types of altars; either of Darkness or of Light. Whether in business, entertainment, sports, politics, science, war, medicine or any other field. We are not merely talking about building a company and turning a profit or hitting the charts for a while, we are talking about world dominion and influence.

Life is spiritual and the physical only takes after the spiritual, in both worlds. There are many drinks in the world but not many are known and craved for globally. Life is spiritual. Everything we see in the natural realm, has its origin in the spirit realm. In other words, the spirit realm is the parent realm. This spiritual principle applies to everything we see including business. It doesn't matter whether you believe it or not, natural endowments can only take you so far. The rest is spirit.

# 20.

## The Hand of God

What makes one person smarter, more successful, taller, stronger, more outgoing, discerning, more cautious or any other trait than the other, right from childhood? One could pose the same question in regards to businesses? What and who makes one business more successful and more preferred or better placed or more influential than the other? Is it all a factor of upbringing and planning? Or is there something more to everything? Navigating the uncertain terrain of life and business often leads us to contemplate the role of unknown forces and the concept of divine intervention, referred to as "the Hand of God" in many cultures. Just as humans face unpredictable events and unforeseen circumstances, businesses too encounter moments of uncertainty and unexpected challenges. There has to be something more.

Despite meticulous planning and preparation, unforeseen events can instantly alter the course of our plans. Businesses may invest heavily in expansion, innovation, and future strategies, yet external factors beyond their control can disrupt these plans.

The wise Chinese philosopher Lao Tzu once said, "Nature does not hurry, yet everything is accomplished," This conveys a message of humility, acknowledging the limits of human control and the influence of unknown forces or divine intervention in shaping outcomes.

Confucius emphasized the need for resilience and preparation, stating, "Success depends upon previous preparation, and without such preparation, there is sure to be failure." This wisdom underscores the importance of being ready for unforeseen events and leveraging preparation to navigate through uncertainties. But this is constantly downplayed by the words of the Psalmist when he says, "Unless the Lord builds the house, its builders labour in vain. Unless the Lord watches over the city, the watchmen stand guard in vain."

We are constantly reminded that our precious plans go astray without God. The Proverbs realign us when they counsel saying, "Trust in the Lord with all your heart and lean not on your own understanding; in all your ways submit to him, and he will make your paths straight."
Italian poet Dante Alighieri reflected on the journey of life, saying, "In His will is our peace." This quote speaks to the peace and assurance found in surrendering to divine will, acknowledging that unknown forces are part of a higher plan that we may not always comprehend.

The interplay between human life and business reveals a shared journey of dependency on unknown forces and divine guidance. Scriptures and much earthly wisdom remind us of the importance of trust, resilience, preparation, and learning from both success and failure in navigating the uncertainties of life and business. Just as humans find solace in the sovereignty of a higher power, businesses can draw strength and wisdom from acknowledging the hand of God as we go along.

Businesses, like human endeavours, often embark on ambitious plans and projects with grand visions of success and prosperity. Like the builders of the biblical Tower of Babel story, aimed to reach the heavens and make a name for themselves, businesses set lofty goals, expansion strategies, and profit targets. However, similar to the disruption faced by the builders of Babel, businesses frequently encounter unforeseen challenges and obstacles that disrupt their carefully laid plans.

The biblical narrative teaches us that human efforts, no matter how well-intentioned or meticulously planned, are subject to the sovereignty of God. In the realm of business, this translates to the recognition that external factors beyond human control can significantly impact outcomes. Economic downturns, natural disasters, technological disruptions, regulatory changes, and global crises are just a few examples of the unpredictable forces that can derail even the most promising business ventures.

The story of the Tower of Babel and its eventual demise serves as a cautionary tale about the dangers of arrogance and self-reliance. Similarly, businesses that operate solely on their own strengths and strategies, without acknowledging the role of divine providence or external factors, may find themselves vulnerable to failure or setbacks. Acknowledging the Hand of God in business endeavours does not diminish the importance of strategic planning, innovation, or hard work. Instead, it reinforces the idea of humility and a broader perspective that factors in spiritual or ethical considerations alongside financial and operational goals.

Business leaders and entrepreneurs who integrate principles of faith, ethical decision-making, and a sense of responsibility toward employees, customers, and society at large are more likely to build resilient and sustainable enterprises. Just as individuals seek divine guidance in their personal lives, businesses can benefit from a mind-set that values integrity, compassion, and a recognition of something greater than mere profit margins.

Citing the Chernobyl Nuclear disaster 1986, The

Climate Change that has deemed the Coal industry a global disadvantage, the Silicon Valley Bank Collapse in 2023, which was one of the most influential and strongest banks responsible for innovation in SV, the unprecedented Dubai Floods in April 2024, which put the Busiest most technologically advanced airport at a halt for days and of course the Covid 19 pandemic (ignoring the mechanics behind it), which caused a global lockdown; these are all a reiteration of the vulnerability of humanity like businesses to God.

In essence, human endeavours, whether in personal or business contexts, are part of a larger narrative shaped by divine providence and interconnected forces. By embracing humility, acknowledging our limitations, and seeking guidance from higher principles, businesses can navigate challenges with greater wisdom, resilience, and ethical clarity, fostering long-term success and a positive impact in the world.

# 21.

## The Contrasts

While businesses and humans share numerous similarities, they also possess distinct differences that stem from their inherent nature, purpose, and capabilities. One fundamental difference lies in their underlying essence. Businesses are entities created by humans to serve specific economic or social purposes, such as generating profits, providing goods and services, or advancing innovation. In contrast, humans are living beings with consciousness, emotions, and intrinsic value beyond their economic contributions.

This distinction underscores the ethical considerations and responsibilities associated with each domain. Another key difference is in their lifespan and sustainability. Businesses can exist for varying durations, from start-ups that may fail within a few years to established corporations that operate for decades or even centuries. Their survival depends on factors such as market conditions, competition, and strategic management. On the other hand, humans have finite lifespans and undergo natural ageing processes that influence their capabilities and experiences over time.

Motivations and decision-making processes also differ between businesses and humans. Businesses are driven by economic goals such as profit maximization, market share growth, and shareholder value creation. Their decisions often revolve around cost-benefit analyses, risk management, and strategic planning to achieve desired outcomes. In contrast, humans are motivated by a complex array of factors including personal values, emotions, relationships, and societal influences. Their decisions encompass moral considerations, emotional well-being, and long-term life goals that extend beyond purely economic considerations.

The nature of relationships and interactions also distinguishes businesses from humans. While businesses engage in transactions, partnerships, and collaborations with other businesses, customers, and stakeholders, these interactions are typically driven by contractual agreements, financial incentives, and business interests. Human relationships, on the other hand, involve emotional connections, empathy, reciprocity, and shared experiences that contribute to social cohesion, personal growth, and well-being.

Responsibilities and accountability differ significantly between businesses and humans. Businesses have legal and ethical obligations to comply with regulations, uphold corporate governance standards, and fulfil their duties to shareholders, employees, customers, and the broader society. They are subject to scrutiny, oversight, and accountability mechanisms that ensure transparency and responsible conduct.

In contrast, humans bear responsibilities towards themselves, their families, communities, and the environment, encompassing ethical behaviour, civic engagement, and sustainable practices that promote collective welfare and environmental stewardship. Finally, the concept of growth and success varies between businesses and humans. While businesses often measure success in terms of financial metrics, market share, and competitive advantages, humans define success in diverse ways that encompass personal fulfilment, meaningful relationships, contributions to society, and overall well-being. The pursuit of happiness, self-actualization, and holistic life satisfaction distinguishes human aspirations from purely economic or materialistic goals.

In essence, while businesses and humans share common ground in their interconnectedness and interactions within society, their inherent differences underscore the multifaceted nature of human existence and the unique roles that businesses play within the broader social and economic landscape. Understanding these differences promotes a balanced perspective that acknowledges both the economic realities of business enterprises and the intrinsic value and dignity of human life.

# Conclusion

Businesses, much like humans, operate within a complex web of relationships, values, and responsibilities. Recognizing these parallels is crucial for leaders, entrepreneurs, and founders as they navigate the dynamic landscape of modern commerce. Viewing businesses through a human lens can provide valuable insights into organizational behaviour, ethical decision-making, and long-term sustainability. Just as individuals have personal values and ethics guiding their actions, businesses should have a strong ethical foundation. Leaders must prioritize integrity, transparency, and accountability in all business dealings. Ignoring ethical considerations can lead to scandals, loss of trust, and legal repercussions, as seen in numerous corporate scandals worldwide.

Human relationships are built on trust, respect, and communication. Similarly, businesses thrive when they prioritize building meaningful relationships with stakeholders—customers, employees, investors, and communities. Neglecting these relationships can result in customer churn, employee disengagement, and reputational damage.

Humans adapt to changing environments, learn from experiences, and innovate to solve problems. Businesses must also be agile and innovative to stay competitive in rapidly evolving markets. Ignoring innovation and clinging to outdated practices can lead to obsolescence and loss of market share.

Just as individuals have social responsibilities towards society, businesses have a responsibility to contribute positively to the communities they operate in. Embracing corporate social responsibility (CSR) initiatives not only benefits society but also enhances brand reputation and attracts socially conscious consumers and investors.

Humans plan for the future, set goals, and work towards achieving them. Similarly, businesses must have a clear long-term vision, strategic planning, and risk management strategies in place.

Ignoring the parallels between businesses and humans can have dire consequences. Leaders who prioritize short-term profits over ethical considerations risk damaging their reputation, losing key talent, facing legal challenges, and ultimately jeopardizing the viability of their businesses. Moreover, in today's interconnected world, where information spreads rapidly through social media and digital platforms, the impact of negative actions can be swift and far-reaching. Therefore, business leaders, entrepreneurs, and founders must pay attention to the human aspects of their organizations. By fostering a culture of ethics, empathy, innovation, and social responsibility, businesses can not only achieve success in the marketplace but also contribute positively to society and leave a lasting legacy of impact and integrity.